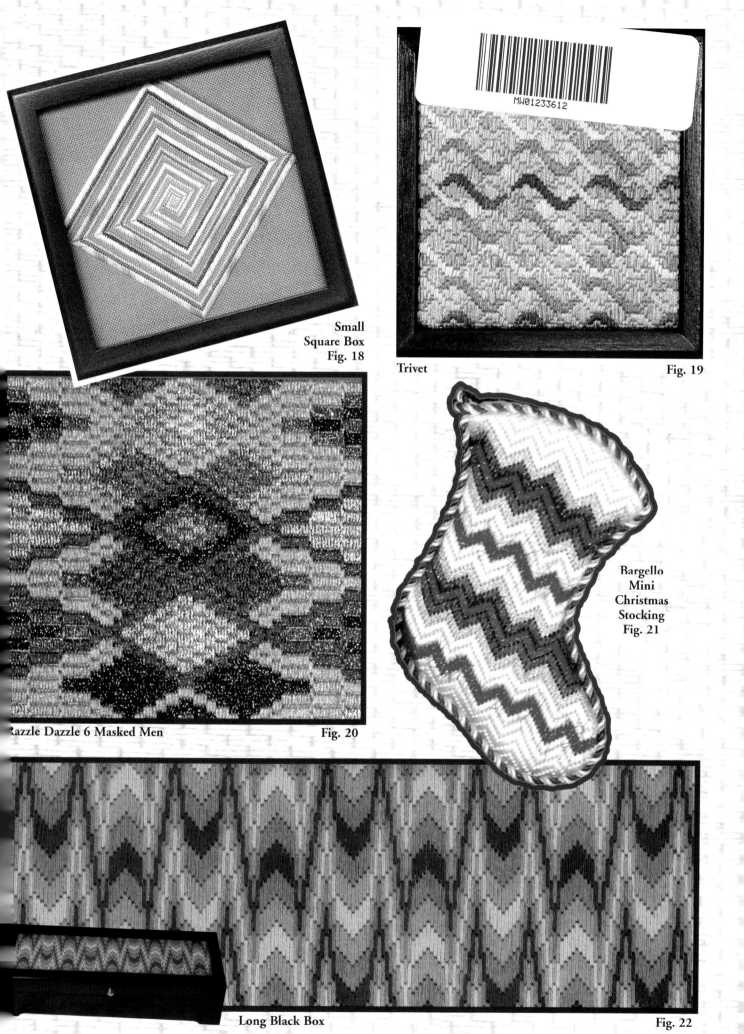

Small
Square Box
Fig. 18

Trivet                                           Fig. 19

Razzle Dazzle 6 Masked Men              Fig. 20

Bargello
Mini
Christmas
Stocking
Fig. 21

Long Black Box                                  Fig. 22

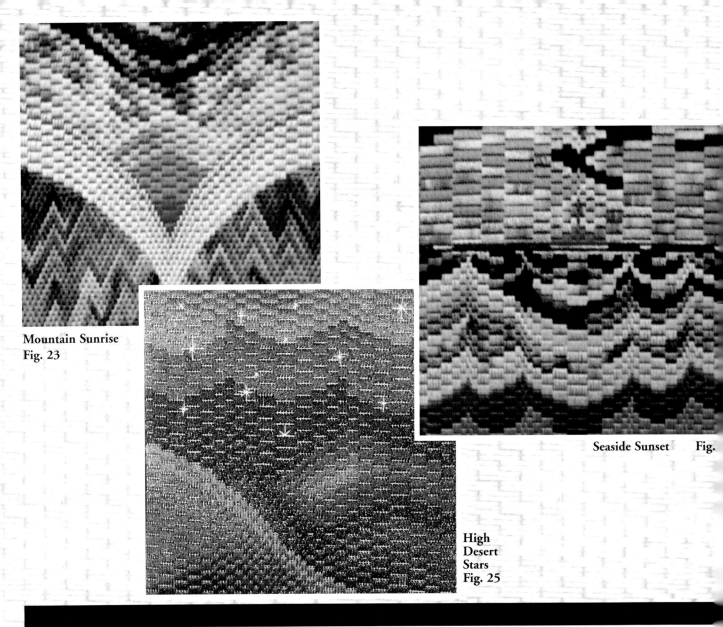

Mountain Sunrise
Fig. 23

Seaside Sunset     Fig.

High
Desert
Stars
Fig. 25

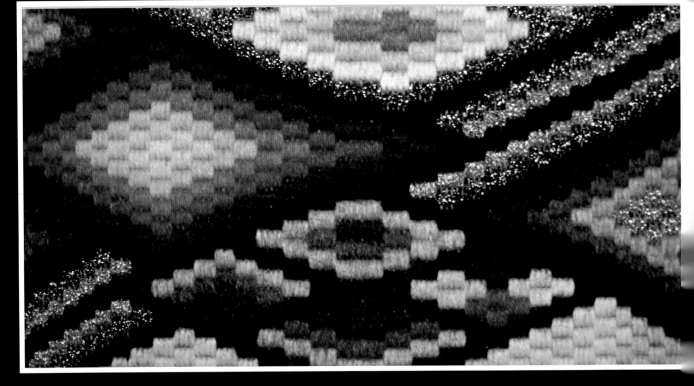

Wings                                                    Fig. 2

# CREATING
# CONTEMPORARY
# *Bargello*
## A DESIGNER'S GUIDE

### *by Iona L. Dettelbach*

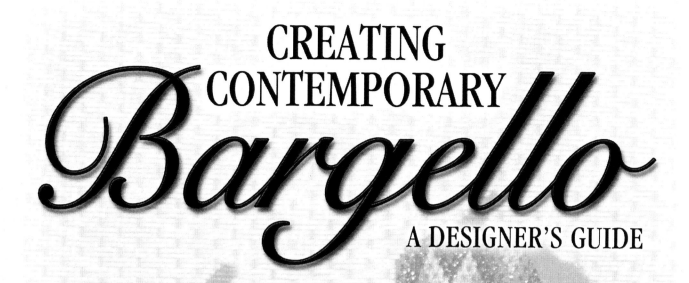

Designed and Stitched by Iona Dettelbach & Susan Seabright

Photography by Larry Osher, DPM

Printed in U.S.A. by Colorbar Perlmuter Printing Company

# Contents

# *Dedication*

This book is dedicated to my very patient husband, Richard. His help has been invaluable. My thanks and love to my daughter Susan Seabright, who devoted countless hours designing and stitching many of the projects in this book. Susan is a consummate artist and an incurable perfectionist. She has a need to figure out how things work, and once that is done, she then tinkers with the rules to create new art forms. You will find her stitching in chapter five, her original designs in chapter six and her finished work pictured in the color sections of the book.

My sincerest appreciation to Dr. Larry Osher who contributed his time, talent, and creativity in photographing and perfecting the charts and photographs that appear in this book.

Thank you to all the wonderful creators of today's beautiful needlework fibers. They have searched the world to bring you the finest materials available. A special thank you to John Schatteles. His urging, support and encouragement, as well as insistence, led to the creation of this book. Thank you to my readers, Carole Arnson, Diane Goldring, Margaret Konecky, Joan Lohr and Sally London. My sincere appreciation to Ruth Dilts for her encouragement and for permission to use her wonderful designs; and to Joan Lohr for forcing me to give up graph paper and colored pencils and enter the computer age. I must also acknowledge my former partner and friend, Kim Cool, who for many years shared with me the dream of writing this book.

Finally, I dedicate this book to all who love stitching. I wish you all many happy hours of creating your own Bargello designs.

Iona L. Dettelbach
Cleveland, Ohio
June, 2007

Copyright ©2007 by Capricorn Designs

Published by Capricorn Designs 2202 Acacia Park Drive Cleveland, Ohio 44124-3865

Printed in USA

ISBN-13-978-0-9792858-0-6
ISBN-10: 0-9792858-0-1
Library of Congress Control Number: 2007901229

# Introduction

My name is Iona Dettelbach and for many years my former partner, Kim Cool, and I owned and ran a needlework shop.

It all began for me over fifty years ago when I noticed a lady stitching something very beautiful. She was seated across from my husband and me in an airport waiting room and was doing a Bargello project. Up to that point in my life I had never tried any decorative stitching. I was captivated! When the plane landed I rushed to a needlepoint shop and purchased my first Bargello project.

In the years since that encounter, I have picked up needle and thread to do many different kinds of needlework, but Bargello is still my favorite.

Bargello is simple to set up on a canvas. All you need to know is how to count carefully. It is the use of color and texture that give Bargello a singular beauty unlike any other needlepoint.

The design concept of Bargello is simple. A pattern *line* of stitches is centered on a canvas. This pattern is repeated over and over until it meets both side borders. The *line* is then repeated below and above the center *line* until the entire canvas is filled. There are many ways to vary the *line* of a design, and this is what we will explore in this book.

If the mechanics of Bargello are simple, the coloring of the canvas is not. There are so many fibers available to today's needle worker that the combinations and possibilities are endless. You will find abundant examples in the color section of this book. A complete description of the fibers used throughout the book can be found in Chapter Seven.

This book is a primer on Bargello design. My aim is to enable you to become a Bargello artist. It is easy to create your own designs once you understand the basic principals of the craft. I have included charted designs which will teach you how to get started. I will discuss color selection. In the color section, you will find illustrations of stitched projects that you may use as a springboard for your own designs. There is a chapter on today's fibers, many of which were used in various projects in the book. My desire is that you will be able to pick up a piece of canvas, some beautiful fibers and create a work of art that is all your own. So settle back and let's begin!

# CHAPTER ONE

## *Supplies, Tools, and Helpful Hints.*

### THE SUPPLIES YOU WILL NEED

Most Bargello projects will be stitched on brown Mono canvas, either with number fourteen (#14) count or number eighteen (#18) count. The count refers to the number of stitches per inch. Do not use interlocked needlepoint canvas for Bargello projects. Most Bargello is worked on brown Mono canvas. The longer straight stitches of Bargello allow an occasional glimpse of the canvas. Brown tends to be less noticeable than white. If you are stitching with white or pastel colors, use white Mono canvas. Needlepoint canvas is an even weave material. Bargello can be stitched on any even weave fabric as long as the threads are adjusted for coverage. You will see examples on the projects and designs featured in the color sections. All the pictured examples are stitched on Zweigart® canvas and even weave fabric. In my opinion, these are the finest products offered to needle workers. You spend much time and effort on your work, so you should use the finest products available. Most shops carry Zweigart canvas and fabrics. The supplies needed for Bargello are listed at the end of this chapter. The canvas and frame sizes will be used in chapter two.

Once you have planned your project and purchased your canvas you will need to mount the canvas on a scroll frame or on stretcher bars. This is absolutely necessary. You cannot create beautiful Bargello designs when stitching in your hand since you will have a hard time controlling the stitch tension. When you use the two handed method of stitching that a frame requires, the stitch tension will be even and your coverage will be perfect.

I own and use the Lowery Workstand, and do most of my Bargello on stretcher bars. You do not have to use a work stand to hold your frame. C clamps will hold your frame to a table. You could also fill bags with play sand and use the weights to hold your frame or stretcher bars to your work surface. I use stretcher bars because I enjoy watching the pattern develop. Of course, if my project is very large, I use a scroll frame.

You will need an assortment of needles. I usually use number twenty needles on a fourteen count canvas and number twenty-two needles on an eighteen count canvas. These needles are one size too large for conventional needlepoint, but they work well for the straight up and down stitching of Bargello and your needles will be easier to thread. Long straight stitches require a slightly thicker thread than other needlepoint stitches. This is another reason for using a slightly larger needle.

You want a good light source and a comfortable chair. You need utility scissors, embroidery scissors, a needle threader and a laying tool for silk, rayon and ribbon. The threader makes your life easier. If you do not own this tool, your needlework shop will sell you one and show you how to use it.

Bargello stitches are long and straight. Twisted threads will show up on the front of your canvas. Using a laying tool while you stitch will eliminate this problem. You do not need an expensive tool for laying threads. You can use a knitting needle or a yarn needle.

My personal favorite is the BLT (Best Laying Tool) by Shay Pendray. It is easy to hold and always cool to the touch. I also own and use a wooden laying tool that is attached to a ring. The ring slips over my wrist and it is easy to flip the tool into my hand when I need it. The ring is worn on the hand that is under the needlework. Most shops carry an assortment of laying tools. Before using the laying tool, place your thread flat on the canvas and straighten the ply (individual threads) by stroking it with your finger.

You are now ready to use the laying tool. When you bring your thread up from the back side of the canvas, put the laying tool down on the canvas and over the thread; then bring your thread down through the canvas to complete the stitch. The thread will run over the laying tool. Remove the tool and tighten the stitch. That is all there is to it. For a little effort you will have a perfect stitch time after time. The process will feel awkward at first, but after a few stitches you will not notice the difference.

We now have a frame, a blank piece of canvas, scissors, needles, a threader and a laying tool. We also need either a staple gun, brass tacks or a roll of stick-on Velcro®. The next step is to cut the canvas with utility scissors. NEVER cut canvas with your embroidery scissors as they will be ruined. Cut the canvas to the size of your project PLUS at least a two inch margin on each side. Thus, if your project is ten inches by ten inches, your canvas will be fourteen by fourteen inches. Next, cover the raw edges of your canvas with masking tape. Mark the center of the canvas with a blue marker that disappears when wet. This marker is available at most needlepoint and quilt shops. To mark the center, measure the canvas both horizontally and vertically. You are looking for the center hole. This is where your design line begins.

Traditionally needle workers use a staple gun or brass tacks to attach the canvas to the stretcher bars. I have begun using stick-on Velcro® tape. You put the fuzzy side on your stretcher bars or on the bars of your scroll frame. The side with the hooks goes on the canvas on top of the masking tape. This is important. If you do not have masking tape on the canvas, it will be damaged when you remove the Velcro®. You can leave the fuzzy tape on your stretcher bars or scroll frame rods if you wish. The hooked tape can be parked on the edge of your frame or, in my case, my work stand. It can be reused several times.

Make sure that the canvas is straight on the rods of your scroll frame or on your stretcher bars. You can insure this by marking the center of your canvas on the top and bottom and marking your bars in the center. By matching the two marks, you will know that the canvas is even. If your scroll frame has bias tapes attached, you will have to sew the canvas to the tapes unless you decide to use the Velcro® sticky tape. In that case, lay the fuzzy Velcro® tape over the staples that hold the bias tape to the bar. Mark the centers as I mentioned above.

It is important that you invest in a good pair of embroidery scissors. Make sure they have small sharp points. If you take care of your scissors and keep them in a sheath or case, they will last you for a lifetime. Your local shop will have a selection from which you can choose.

By now you might have noticed that, we as yet, have no pattern. In Bargello you can put the cart before the horse. It does not matter which comes first, the pattern or the project. Since you are working with a mathematical pattern, it can be adjusted to fit anything. I very often have no idea of where my project will end up or what it will be. On the other hand, I often buy an item that I plan to embellish with Bargello and do know how large my canvas must be. For now, I would like you to equip yourself with all the items listed below. Cut a fourteen by fourteen inch piece of fourteen count brown Mono canvas, and find some leftover Persian wool, or any other similar weight material. This is going to be a doodle canvas for you to use as you learn about the heart of any Bargello project, the design line.

**The list of supplies that we discussed is as follows:**

☐ 14" x 14" Brown Mono 14 Count Canvas.

☐ 14" x 14" Stretcher Bars, or a Scroll Frame and bars to hold a 14"x 14" canvas.

☐ Velcro Tape®, tacks or a staple gun & staples.

☐ Utility Scissors

☐ Assortment of fibers as discussed

☐ Needles, sizes 20 & 22

☐ Embroidery Scissors

☐ Masking Tape

☐ Blue Quilters Pen

☐ Colored Pencils

# CHAPTER TWO
## *Getting Started*

### BASIC BARGELLO INSTRUCTIONS

There are two types of Bargello patterns, Hungarian and Florentine. The history associated with these is shrouded in mystery. Even the two names are a point of contention among the early authors of Bargello books. I will follow the lead of the majority of the Bargello historians. One thing that everyone agrees with is that all traditional Bargello stitches are straight stitches that lay vertically on the canvas. In typical Florentine point, stitch patterns cover four threads of the canvas with a step up or down of two threads. Follow this progression in the first illustration below. This is a typical chevron pattern.

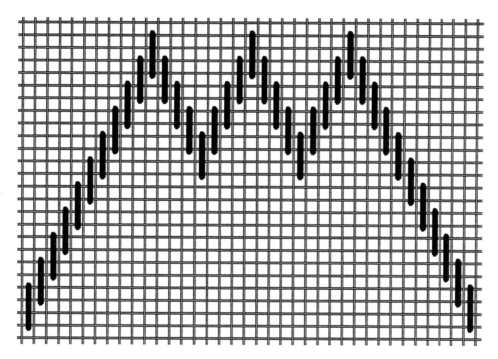

*Florentine Point Pattern*

The second illustration is of the Florentine arch or curve. The curve is accomplished by using groups or bundles of stitches. At the top of the arch, you will see a bundle of four stitches, followed by a bundle of three stitches, two bundles of two stitches and three single stitches in descending order. I will discuss this fully later in the chapter.

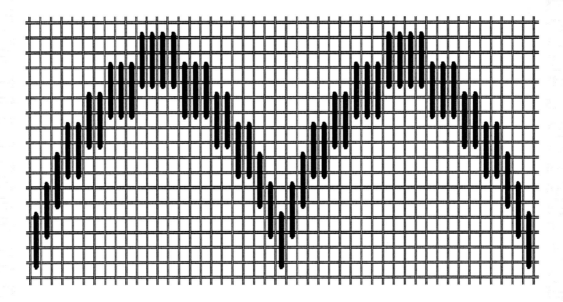

*Florentine Arch Pattern*

The third illustration on the following page is a typical Hungarian Point pattern. A stitch can cover as many as six threads or as few as two. The stitches are typically, but not always, arranged in groups of two long stitches followed by two short stitches. The step up and down is usually one thread. This grouping of long and short stitches produces a unique secondary pattern. You will discover this in the projects that deal with Hungarian Point patterns. The pattern that I used to illustrate Hungarian Point is found on a chair that is displayed in the National Museum in Florence, Italy. This museum was once a prison called the Bargello. Bargello in Italian means "Constable." Some say that this is how Bargello needlework earned its name even though the chairs appeared after the prison became a museum. What is interesting is the fact that one of the oldest known examples of the Hungarian Point stitch method is found in Florence, Italy while the origins of the Florentine Point method is said to be Hungary. So now we have another Bargello mystery.

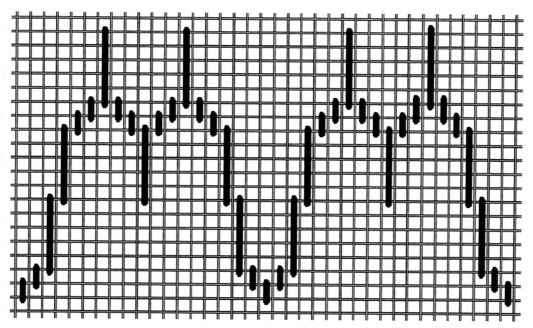

*Hungarian Point Pattern*

Study the three patterns. They are similar but quite different. Since Hungarian point is slightly more complicated for the beginning designer/stitcher, we will deal with this method in a later chapter. All illustrations in this chapter show the Florentine method. The basic instructions for successful Bargello projects are the same for both types.


## STITCHING BASIC BARGELLO

*This is a note to those already familiar with needlepoint. Take the time to read through the following suggestions. I have been stitching for over fifty years and I still learn new things all the time; usually from students.*

Readers should take the doodle canvas prepared in chapter one and stitch the illustrations which are on the next page.

The method that you use to place stitches is very important when stitching Bargello. You cannot be economical with your thread at the expense of the beauty of your stitches. Follow the method as illustrated. The odd numbers signify the beginning of each stitch or the point where the needle comes up from the back of the canvas. The second illustration shows you *what not to do*. If your stitches are placed side by side in that manner they will roll away from each other and expose too much canvas.

After you have stitched the "correct method of stitching", look at the back of your canvas. Using the correct method gives you shorter stitches as you progress down the diagonal areas of the design. Since these stitches lie diagonally on the back of the canvas, they will be secure. If you follow this method, you will have long stitches on the back of the canvas when stitching the "bundles" of three, and shorter diagonal stitches covering two threads when traveling down the diagonal line. Traveling up the diagonal line produces longer diagonal stitches. The short diagonal stitches on the back provide you with a good place for ending threads. Go under several long stitches, then under a few shorter, tighter stitches to secure the tail of the thread.

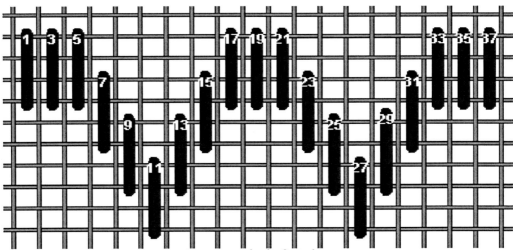

*Correct method of stitching*

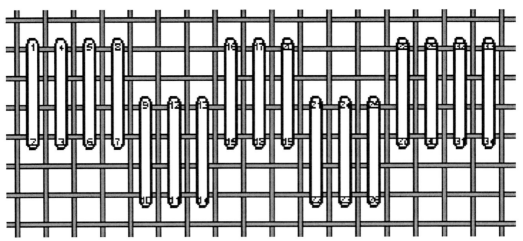

*Wrong method of stitching*

If you have stitched the examples above you should be able to see the difference in the look of your stitching. Do not worry about running out of thread on a Bargello project. Since the colors are usually separated, which you will discover in the chapter on color, it does not matter if dye lots are different. However, you should start a line of stitches with enough thread to finish that line. This is where dye lot differences will be evident. As you read on in this chapter you will find out how to estimate how much fiber you will need.

## PLACING A BARGELLO PATTERN IN THE CENTER OF THE CANVAS

Bargello patterns are usually started at the exact middle of the canvas and they expand evenly to the borders. There are exceptions, but you will not meet up with them until the section on Free Form Bargello. Since Bargello is stitched in the holes between the canvas threads, you count holes to find the horizontal and vertical center of the canvas. However, the stitches do go over canvas threads. Therefore you count threads when stitching the steps up and down the pattern. Let me illustrate.

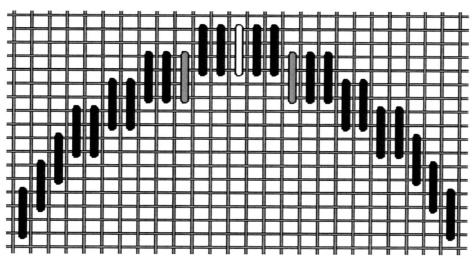

*Centering the design*

The white stitch is at the center of the canvas. The stitch lies in the <u>holes</u> in the center of the canvas. The black stitches on either side complete that section of the pattern. The grey stitches on either side of the center section are the first stitches down. The step down is two <u>threads</u>. All Bargello patterns, whether Hungarian or Florentine operate in this manner. When you are finding the exact center of your canvas, you are looking for those lines of holes in the center. These lines will be vertical and horizontal in the form of a cross. When you are talking about the steps up or down that make up your pattern, you are talking about threads. If you understand this, you understand Bargello.

Here is an important rule and a hint that will help. All traditional Bargello patterns proceed across the canvas in a symmetrical way. If you constantly check the top and bottom stitches of your pattern you cannot make a mistake. If you do find an error and, if you are like me, you will on occasion; you must fix it immediately. It is impossible to correct a Bargello pattern if it has gone wrong for a row or two. You will have to remove stitches back to the error in order to continue. Look at the illustration on the next page. The grey stitches indicate where you should be checking to see if the pattern is correct. This is especially important when stitching the first row. This row is the design line and is the heart of your pattern.

## CHECKING FOR ERRORS

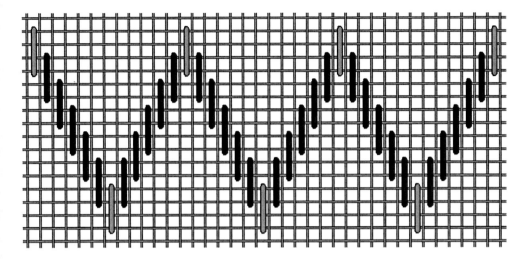

*Checking For Errors*

Take out your practice canvas and stitch the illustration above. If you have done this exercise successfully you know how to stitch a Bargello design.

Before you start stitching, let's discuss estimating the amount of material you will need to complete a design. Once you have decided on your pattern, and the number of colors you will use, buy one skein or card of each color. Stitch as much as you can of one quarter of the pattern. Since Bargello is a repetition of lines in a pattern, you can now estimate your needs to finish the project.

Up to now, the illustrations we have discussed and stitched are all basic Bargello design lines. There are many variations available to the Bargello artist. It's time to learn some of those variations.

## THE DESIGN LINE

All Bargello patterns; Hungarian, Florentine, Four Way or Free Form are derived from a Design Line. This is the first line you lay down on the canvas to set the pattern. Traditional Bargello design lines have been a part of the needle workers repertoire for centuries. They are all the same and at the same time all different. This is part of the charm of Bargello stitching. Every needle artist interprets similar elements in their own way. The constraints of space, different tastes in colors and unusual interpretations of descending and ascending lines all lend originality to a basic design. The designs in this book and other Bargello books illustrate how different interpretations of Bargello design lines have influenced the creativity of all needlework artists.

## CHEVRON PATTERN VARIATIONS

Chevron patterns are the simple first steps in Bargello design. The steps up and down can be varied by any count but it is best to keep these steps in odd numbers as it is easier to halve them when adding other elements. You will see what I mean in the third example. These first three design lines illustrated below are one; a simple chevron line, two; a mirror image chevron line and three; a woven chevron design line. The fourth and fifth design lines on the next page are a combination of chevrons at different heights. As exercise one, stitch these five design lines.

*Chevron Design Lines One, Two and Three*

This illustration combines Chevrons of different lengths.

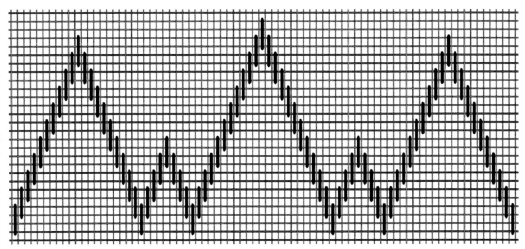

*Design Line Four-Chevrons of Different Lengths*

## DIAGONAL DESCENDING CHEVRONS

Look at the small chairs in color figure 32 on the back cover. This pattern appears in red and white on the chair at the left in the photograph.

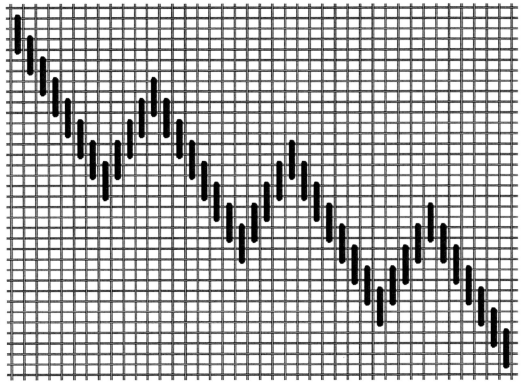

*Design Line Five-Descending Chevrons*

## THE BARGELLO CURVE

The curved line in a Bargello pattern is a lovely design element. The height and the width of the curve is dictated by the number of descending double bundles and single stitches that are used. If this seems confusing don't worry, there are examples below.

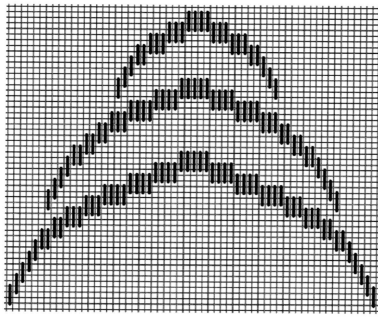

*Different Size Arches*

In the illustration above there are three arches. In the top arch, the smallest, there is a bundle of four stitches followed by two bundles of three, one bundle of two and three single stitches in descending order. To create the wider middle arch, we begin with a bundle of five, followed by two bundles of four, one bundle of three, three bundles of two and four descending single stitches. For the large arch, we added one bundle of four, one bundle of three and one additional single stitch. You can see that the more bundles you add to your arch, the wider it will be. The more single stitches that descend after the last bundle, the steeper the arch will be.

In the second illustration on the following page we see a row of arches followed by the mirror image of the first row of arches. The third element is the ribbon which is formed by inverting the center design line. Below that, I have combined three rows of mirror imaged arches to form a complete pattern. Notice the interesting curved diamonds that are created. This is a secondary pattern. Most mirror images create some sort of secondary pattern. This is one of the things that makes designing Bargello so interesting, and the results so beautiful. Note also that the two secondary diamonds are slightly different. This is because the second row of circles was joined below the bundle of four and the third row of circles shares the bundle of four. I know this sounds confusing, but if you stitch the second exercise found on the next page, you will see what I mean.

*Exercise Two*
*Arches, Ovals, Ribbon and overall design*

Once we have worked with arches and chevrons we can see how these two elements look when they are combined. This was the first pattern I stitched many years ago. Would you like to try to fill this in on your own? If not, the last illustration will give you an example of what I might do. Remember, there is no right or wrong way to color in a pattern. This is the most interesting part of Bargello design, and we will discuss this thoroughly in the chapter *The Soul of Bargello*.

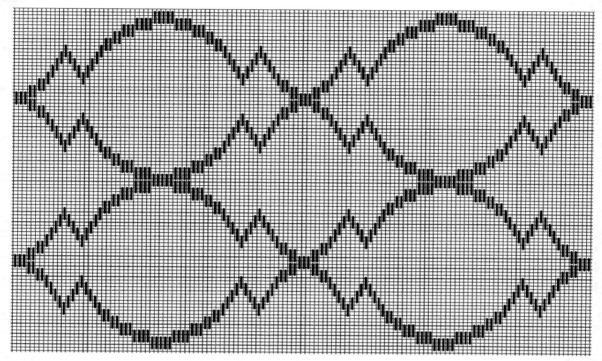

*Mirrored Image Chevrons and Curves*

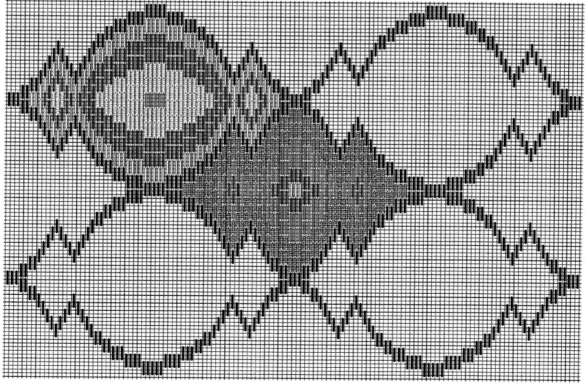

*Iona's Color Scheme*

# CHAPTER THREE
## *Background Stitches that Compliment Bargello*

Several of the projects in this book employ needlepoint stitches as backgrounds to Bargello motifs. This is true of the project pictured on the cover. Almost any straight stitch compliments and blends easily with Bargello patterns. Basketweave stitches fit anywhere on any canvas. Backgrounds should be stitched in one color that highlights the colors used in your pattern. The following stitches are favorites of mine. You can find many others in one of the excellent books of stitches available to needlepoint enthusiasts. Many straight stitches produce strong patterns. Make sure that your choice of stitch does not overpower your Bargello motif. Most of these stitches can be lengthened. Lengthening a stitch will shorten the time devoted to working your background. If you do increase the length of your stitch, you will most likely have to increase the thickness of the fiber in your needle.

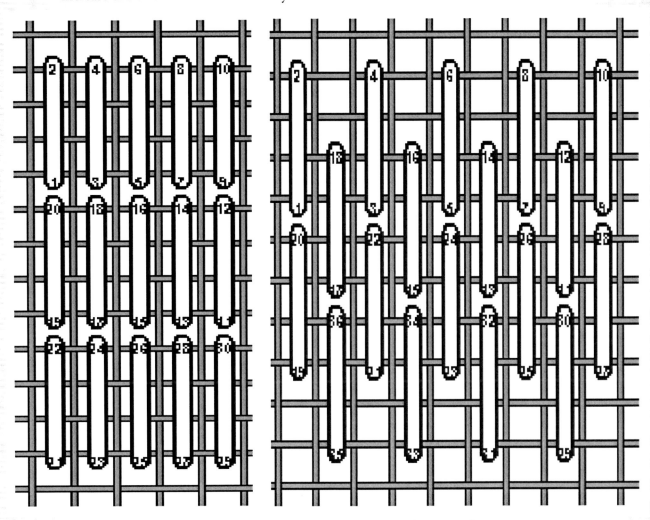

*Straight Gobelin*                    *Giant Brick*

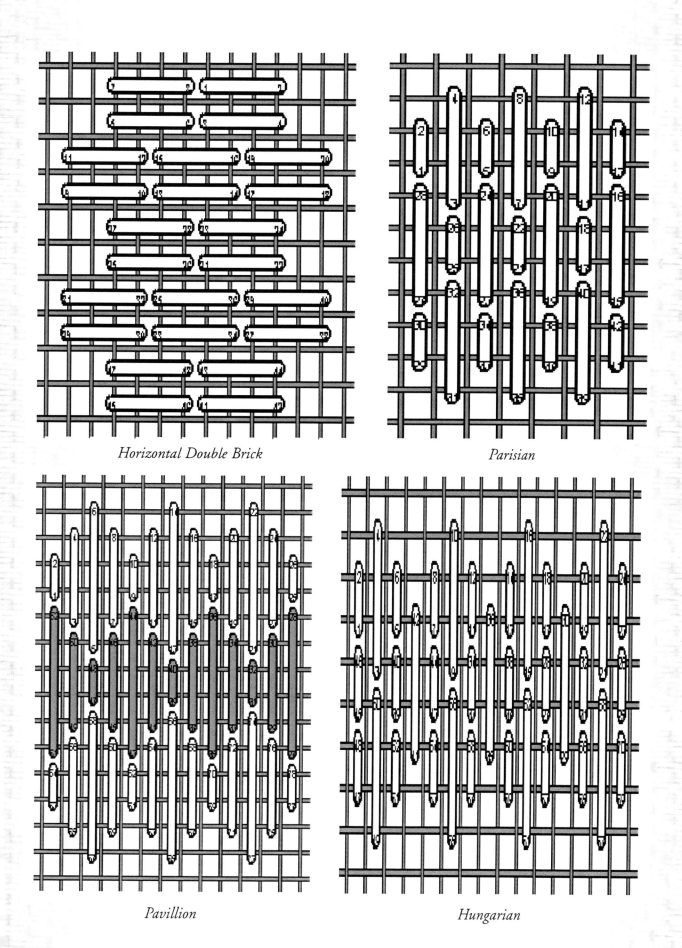

*Horizontal Double Brick*

*Parisian*

*Pavillion*

*Hungarian*

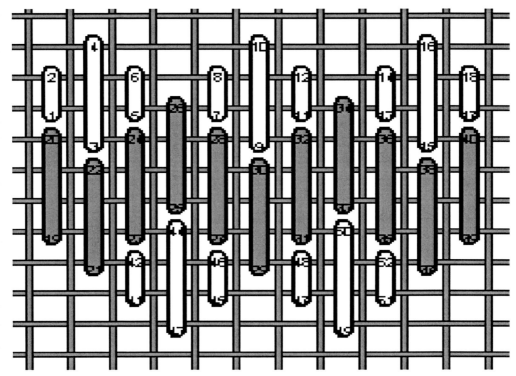

*Hungarian Ground*

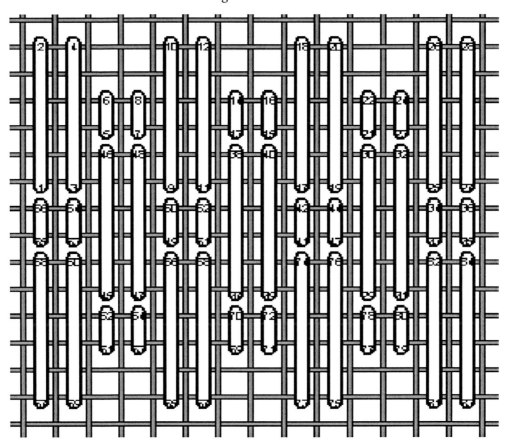

*Old Florentine*

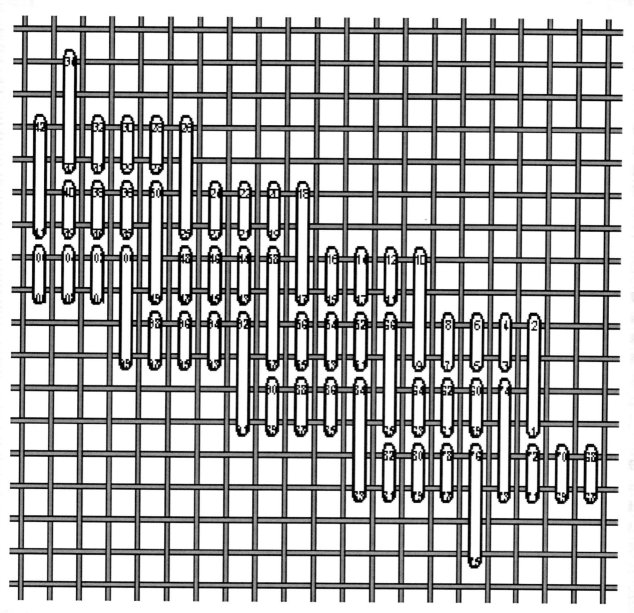

*Victorian Step*

# CHAPTER FOUR

# The Heart of Bargello Design

## THE DESIGN LINE

All Bargello designs, whether complicated or simple, begin with one line - the design line. This horizontal line sets the pattern that is the heart of Bargello design. In most traditional patterns, this line is consistent throughout the entire project.

In the illustration below, you will find a basic chevron pattern. The design line is in black and its center stitch is shown in white. The shading lines are in two shades of gray. I have included the shading lines in this pattern so that you can see how the design line influences all lines above and below it.

Find the white stitch in the illustration below. Then scan that line horizontally from side to side. You will see that all the large and small peaks are in the same line. The illustrations on the next pages are all variations of the chevron pattern and show only the black design line. We will save shading for the chapter on color.

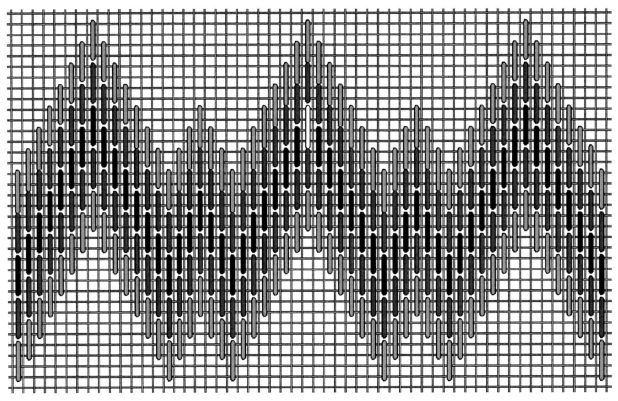

*Basic Chevron Pattern with Shading*

The next illustrations show the same design line in a mirror image pattern. The mirror image appears in grey. Notice that we now have large and small diamonds in our design. Mirror image two illustrates a second way to style the chevron line. In the first example the lowest stitch is shared. In design two, the bottom stitches each have their own space. The diamonds are now one stitch larger and are elongated and wider. In Bargello design, the insertion of a single stitch can make a great difference.

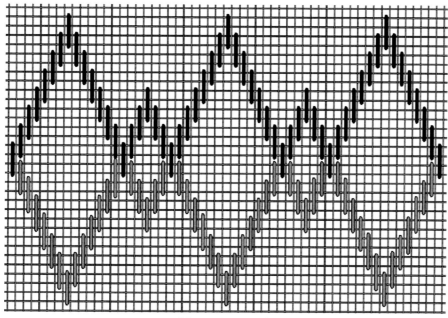

*Mirror Image One*

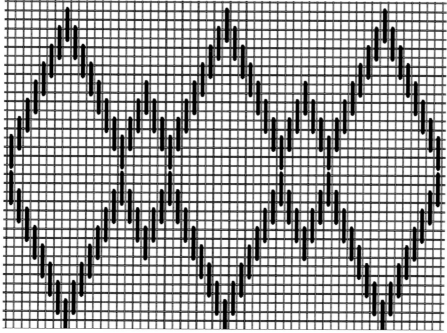

*Mirror Image Two*

Another variation in design is the overlay. The first illustration is the basic chevron design. In the second illustration, the design line is repeated to create a two-color chevron pattern. The second line is shown in grey and is placed half way between the peaks of the original black design line. This pattern must contain an odd number of stitches on the descending and ascending lines so that the stitches will divide evenly.

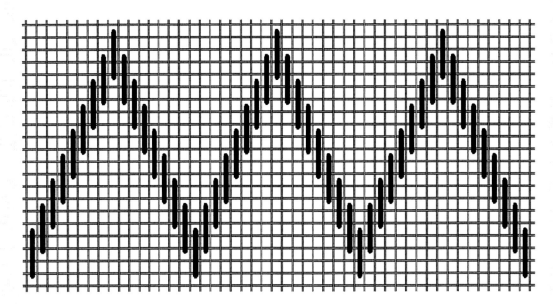

*Basic Chevron Design*

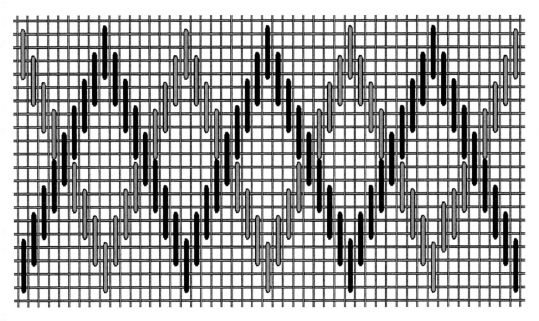

*Two Color Chevron Overlay*

So far we have seen design lines that travel across the canvas. But a design line can also travel diagonally up and down the canvas. This example is the same pattern that you saw in chapter two, but the right leg of the chevron has been extended to travel diagonally from the top to the bottom of the canvas. When you choose to do a diagonal pattern that will be simply shaded, you do not need to center the design. Just start at the top and work down.

If you are doing a more complicated design, you will want to start in the center and work up and then down in order to achieve a symmetrical pattern. This pattern has been worked and mounted on the left small chair in color figure 32 on the back cover. It is the Florentine Point version of the flame stitch.

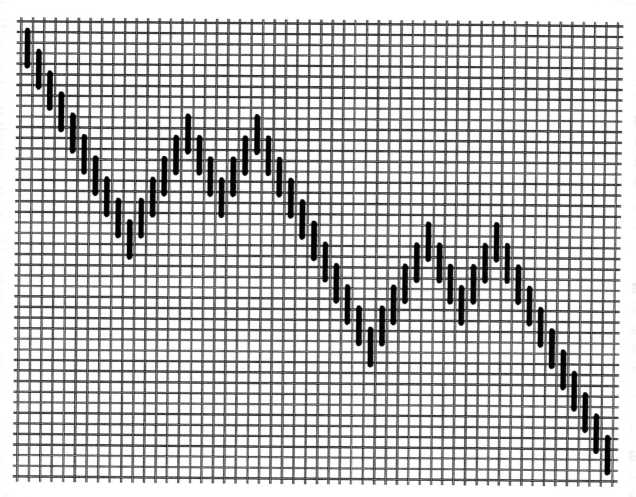

*Diagonal Chevron*

Now let's see how chevron design lines look when they are expanded into an all over pattern. Here is a completed Bargello pattern layout. Complete that is, except for the color. The design lines are the bare bones of Bargello. They are the maps around which you will build your own creations.

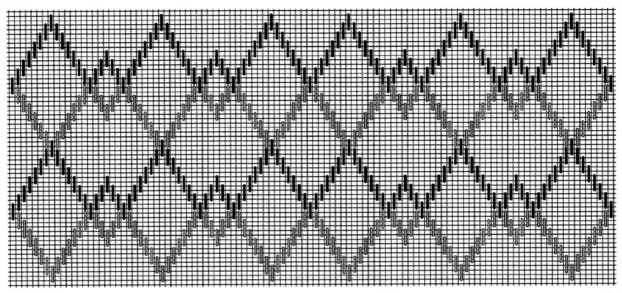

*Mirror Image One expanded*

When the Mirror Image One design is expanded, an additional motif, the double pointed diamond appears. Study this design and stitch Mirror Image Two on your doodle canvas. We will use this in our chapter on color. Follow the diagram below. The design is 109 holes wide by 36 threads high. You will need an area of canvas 3 inches high and 8 inches wide since you are using canvas that has fourteen threads to the inch.

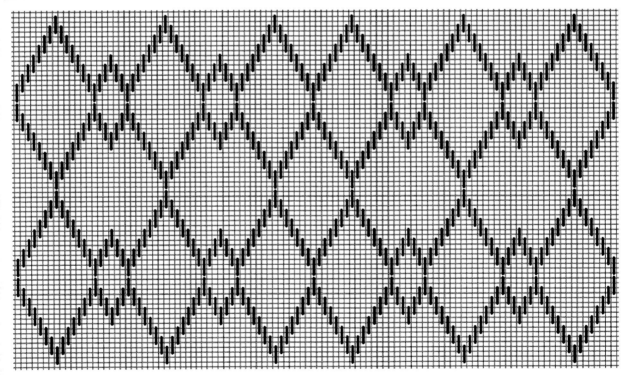

*Mirror Image Two Expanded*

We have only covered a portion of the possibilities. Bargello is not all jagged edges. Many beautiful designs feature the Bargello curved line and combinations of chevrons and curves. The next design lines are made up of curves. These can be rigid lines much like the chevrons. These design lines can also be mirror imaged or half dropped. Curved lines can be reversed to form undulating ribbons. When curves are combined with chevrons they form some of the most beautiful historic Bargello designs.

## CURVED BARGELLO DESIGN LINES

The Bargello Curve is formed by bundles of straight stitches. Look at the illustration below. At the top of the curve is a "bundle" of five stitches. This bundle will determine the size and depth of the curve. Follow the stitches down one side of the curve. The bundle of five is followed by three bundles of four stitches, two bundles of three stitches, two bundles of two stitches and finally, five single stitches. I have created a very wide arch. Watch what happens when I change the count of the stitch bundles. In the bottom example we have one bundle of five stitches, followed by one of four and one bundle of three stitches; two bundles of two stitches and five single stitches. The upper bundles of five, four and three stitches determine the width of the arch. The bundles of two and one determine the depth of the arch.

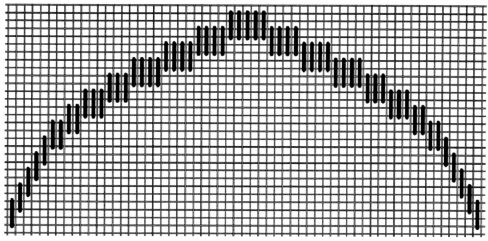

*Wide Bargello Arch*

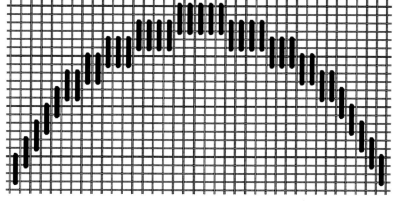

*Narrow Bargello Arch*

The third illustration is of the mirror image that produces a circle or an oval. The oval is formed when the lowest stitch is shared. The circle is formed when each half of the design has its' own beginning stitch. There is no perfect circle in Bargello as there is no perfect circle in any other form of needlepoint.

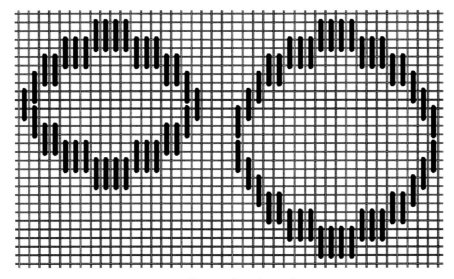

*Bargello Oval and Circle*

There are many lovely ways to use curved lines in a Bargello design. The illustration below is of the narrow arch in mirror image. The illustration on the following page is the narrow arch reversed to form a ribbon design line. The third illustration is the narrow arch reversed and overlayed to form a woven two-ribbon design line. You will notice that the light line goes over and then under the dark line to form the weave.

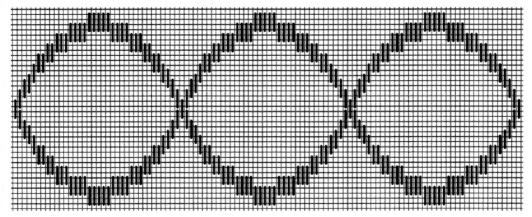

*Narrow Arch Mirror Image*

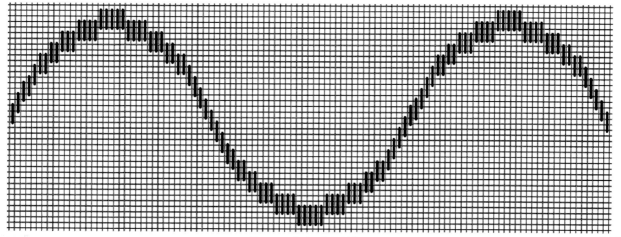

*Reversed Arch Ribbon*

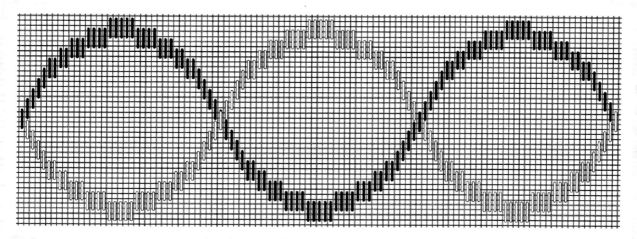

*Overlayed Reversed Arch with Two Woven Ribbons*

In the design below we have combined the arch and the chevron. The illustration on the following page is the same design line in mirror image. Below that is the expanded design of the mirrored image.

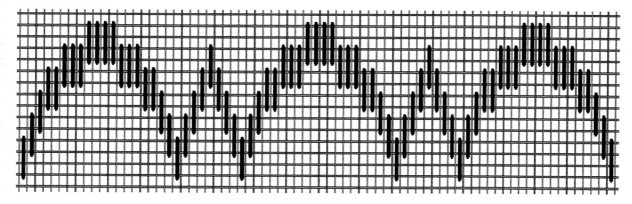

*Arch and Chevron*

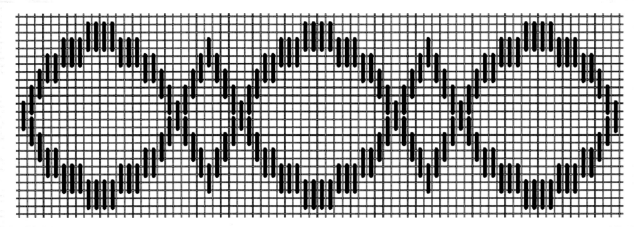

*Mirror Image Arch and Chevron*

## EXPANDING THE DESIGN

This expanded pattern is very unique. The arches form ovals and the chevrons create four separate diamonds, two that are small and two that are flared. Stitch this design on your canvas. We will use it in the chapter on shading. If you do not remember how to estimate the space needed, go back to the chevron expansion explanation.

*Expanded Mirror Image Arch and Chevron*

## HUNGARIAN BARGELLO PATTERNS

Hungarian patterns are quite different than Florentine patterns. At first glance they look more difficult than the preceding patterns. The long stitch usually covers six threads. The short stitch usually covers two threads. The step up and down is one thread. The long and short stitches always produce a secondary background pattern which is quite pleasing. The problem is that if your pattern goes wrong, it is very evident. Below is a typical Hungarian design line. I will follow it with a shaded pattern because it is impossible to guide you through Hungarian Bargello without multiple lines. Before you start to stitch, take a good look at the chart on the next page. Notice the Chevron pattern formed by the short and long stitches. This is one way of finding your way as you stitch. A second way is the knowledge that the next stitch is one thread above or below the last one. The third way is perhaps the best. If you follow one line of stitches vertically down the canvas, you will see that there is a pattern of two short stitches followed by two long stitches all the way down the row. There are several different patterns of Hungarian Point in the projects that follow this chapter. They all have a similar pattern path. Always remember that the step is one up or one down. Check your stitch. If it does not step up or down by one to the stitch next to it, the stitch is incorrect and needs to be removed. Do this immediately. Hungarian Point is even harder to correct than Florentine Point if it goes wrong.

One fact is important to remember about Hungarian Point patterns. They are very hard to mirror image and impossible to overlay.

On the next few pages I have given you a few Hungarian design lines to work with. If you have trouble visualizing the pattern, sketch it out on the graph paper you will find in this book or at your favorite craft store. Sketching it out will help you make sense of the pattern as well as provide you with a map to follow. Use your colored pencils.

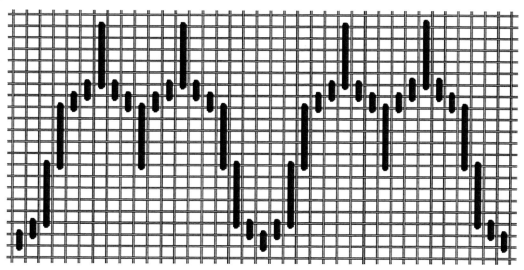

*A Typical Hungarian Design Line*

The shaded Hungarian design below clearly shows the patterns formed by the long and short stitches. If you stitch this simple pattern, you will understand the guiding principles of Hungarian Point Bargello. You can stitch this pattern using only one color, and you will still achieve the distinctive look of this lovely form of Bargello.

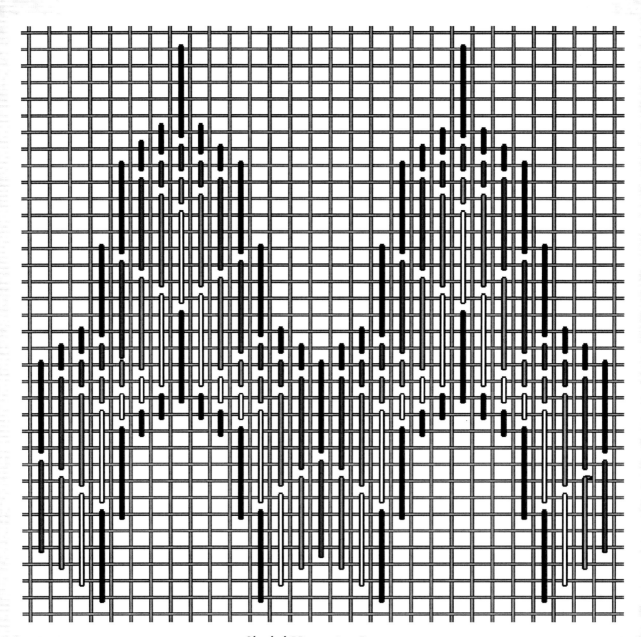

*Shaded Hungarian Pattern*

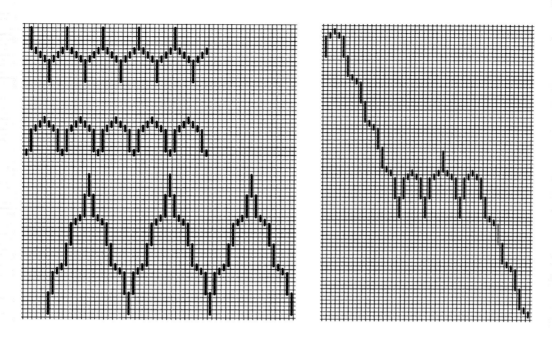

## HUNGARIAN POINT DESIGN LINES

Now that we have touched on Hungarian Point Bargello and have the ability to expand Bargello patterns, it is time to color in the patterns we have stitched. If you have not done any stitching yet, that is not a problem. Just follow these steps. Make sure to start with at least two inch margins on the edge of the canvas. This way if your design shifts a bit you will not run out of space. To recap, take any design line and do one of these things:

1. For a **straight up and down design**; center the design line both vertically and horizontally and repeat the same line above and below the center in the colors you choose. (This will duplicate the first illustration in this chapter.).

2. For a **mirror image design**; find the exact center of the canvas and stitch your design line. Create a mirror image of the design line and stitch. Repeat the mirror image above and below the original until you have filled the desired area. In the next chapter we will color this design.

3. For a **diagonal design**; start at an upper corner of the canvas and stitch your diagonal design line. In the next chapter, we will add the colors you have chosen.

Once you have done this, you are ready for the next chapter and the fun part of stitching Bargello, coloring in the design.

# CHAPTER FIVE
## *The Soul of Bargello Design*

### COLOR:

The basic geometrics of Bargello have been set. Now we are ready for the drama. We all have favorite colors and color combinations. If you are an active needlepointer, you most likely have a quantity of threads on hand. If you do not have left over threads, buy one skein each of four shades and tints in two of your favorite colors, eight skeins total. On the following pages, I am going to show you several different ways of filling in linear patterns, diamonds and ovals. After you have studied these pages, you should be able to fill in the expanded patterns that you stitched on your doodle canvas. If you have already taken the "Chevrons and Curves" challenge from Chapter Two, you are one step ahead. Congratulations!

Before we begin, let's talk a bit about color. You may be familiar with a color wheel. I will review the basic principals of color. Colors are actually light rays filtered from the sun through our atmosphere. These rays travel to us in three primary colors; red, blue and yellow. Look at the color wheel illustrated below. The primary colors are shown in **bold** type. Notice that you could draw a triangle between them. These three primary colors are pure color and can not be mixed by combining other colors.

The three primaries can combine to produce three secondary colors. The secondary colors are <u>underlined</u> on the color wheel. Red and blue combined in equal amounts make violet; yellow and red make orange, and blue and yellow make green. Like the primaries, the secondary colors can also be linked by a triangle. When the two triads are complete they are the source for all the colors that exist.

**Yellow**

*Yellow Orange*          *Yellow Green*

<u>Orange</u>          <u>Green</u>

*Red Orange*          *Blue Green*

**Red**          **Blue**

*Red Violet*          *Blue Violet*

<u>Violet</u>

For example, a primary and a secondary color combine to produce the tertiary colors. These colors are red orange, yellow orange, yellow green, blue green, blue violet and red violet. The tertiary colors are shown in *italics* on the wheel on page 36. When all these colors are arranged in a wheel, one has the basic working tool for figuring out a color scheme. The color wheel represents the first dimension of color which is hue.

The second dimension of color is value. This is where black and white enter the picture. Black is the absence of all color and white is the presence of all colors. Browns are created by mixing two primaries and a secondary. Grays are mixtures of black and white. To create a warm gray, yellow or red is added; to create a cool gray, blue or green is added.

Artists do not go out to the backyard to capture light rays. Painters buy paint that is made up of pigments that display the color traits. You are a fiber artist and the same pigments that painters buy for their pictures are used to dye your threads. Therefore, the same color theories apply.

Yellow, Yellow Orange, Orange, Red Orange, Red, Red Violet and Violet are next to each other on the wheel and form the monochromatic warm color scheme. Blue Violet, Blue, Blue Green, Green and Yellow Green on the opposite side of the wheel form the cool monochromatic color scheme. These monochromatic colors are very beautiful when used in Bargello designs. They blend together in a smooth moiré field.

Colors that are opposites on the color wheel create vibrating color combinations that are very vivid. Think about Christmas Red and Christmas Green. Both at full intensity vibrate with holiday cheer. In addition, one side of the wheel, Blue, Green and Violet are cool restful colors while the opposite side, Red, Orange and Yellow are warm colors and are lively and bright. The warm colors stand out while the cool colors stay in the background. Look at a landscape. You will see misty grey-blue mountains and subdued green forests. But the canoe traveling down the bright blue river, highlighted with glints of white, will be red or yellow. The artist does this to create depth in the painting and you can also do this with your color selection.

This is the time to discuss "tints and shades". This is what I meant when I mentioned the moiré method of shading Bargello. Take the color red. A true artists' color is cadmium red, which refers to the source material that creates the color. Cadmium red is a bright vivid color. It's value is pure, and if you were going to paint a red rose, this is what you would do: First you would create your palate by placing a squeeze of red, one of black and one of white at equal distances on the palate. The lightest colors are tints and are the highest in value, or brightness. They are created by adding white. The opposite is true of the darker colors which are called shades and are created by adding black. The intensity of color tends to recede when lowered or darkened. Colors that are lightened will tend to come forward. Actually nothing in nature is just one color. Look at an apple. It is a perfect example of what I am talking about. Apples look red or green or even yellow. They look that way but they are not. Even the good old one color orange is not all orange if you look at it closely. That is why needlepoint canvases are painted in many colors. Even though the Bargello projects we will be doing are not a classic shaded picture canvas, you can still be guided by following the basic principles of color. The fact that I was an easel painter before painting needlepoint canvases has been invaluable to me when planning my own projects. That is why I wanted you to have a quick overview of color theory. If you are interested in learning more, you will find many books on the subject in your local library or bookstore.

The nice thing about being a needle artist is that you do not have to mix the colors yourself. You have seen the multitude of colors hanging on the walls or arranged in the drawers at your local shop. Colors are usually arranged in "families" of several tints and shades. When coloring a conventional painted needlepoint canvas, the artist rarely uses more than three shades or tints of a family. That is because many needlepointers could have a hard time distinguishing more than that. This is not the case in Bargello. You can easily use the wonderful families of six or seven colors in a moiré shading scheme. Let's assume that you have chosen a seven shaded and tinted color family. The true color would be your design line; the three tints would be arranged from darkest to lightest above the design line and the three shades would be arranged from lightest to darkest below the design line.

As you progress, you will be creating designs with secondary patterns. The way you color the secondary patterns will have a lot to do with the over-all look of your design. Say that you do a design line in metallic gold, and then color the principal pattern in bright reds. If you choose bright greens for your secondary design, you would have a Christmas canvas. If you choose red-oranges and red-browns, you would have a fall canvas. Blues and whites speak of the sea shore while light grays and antique blues feel like winter. Yellow and yellow-greens are the colors of spring.

Use this information for creating your own Bargello designs. First, decide if your project will be cool or bright, or a combination of both. Decide if you will use several shades and tints of the same color for the moiré look, or if you will be using bright opposing primary colors that will shout "hey, look at me". Will your colors share the same side of the color wheel and blend smoothly, or will they be opposites on the wheel and vibrate?

This is how I go about planning the color design, whether working with leftovers or buying new threads. I select the fibers and colors that I will use. Then I lay each skein on a flat surface and step away. What I see on the table is what my color design will look like when it is stitched. Looking through slightly narrowed eyes, I can determine whether a color is out of line or if all colors selected blend together. If you are really undecided about colors, take the threads outside in the natural light. Artificial light affects colors and does not give you a true picture of your selections.

In the old days of needlework, fibers were usually some type of wool. In today's world, there is a vast array of wonderful fibers to choose from. We will discuss this in the chapter on fibers, but I would like to mention one result of all this variety. Texture has now become a factor in Bargello design.

Different fibers reflect color in different intensities. For example, silk and rayon reflect light at a greater intensity than other fibers. Today's metallic threads are usually polymers and will not tarnish, remaining bright and shiny forever. Ribbon threads, being flatter than round threads also reflect light differently. The same is true of the "fuzzy" fibers that add so much texture to a design. When you are planning projects, take time to look at several different types of thread. Consider combining several varieties in one design.

You have now reached the charted section of this book. The charts are easy to follow. The design lines are in black when possible. The color used is designated in the color key as the design line. When it comes to color, the following charts are just suggestions. Feel free to change them. After you have looked at the chart, take a piece of canvas and try stitching the diamonds. This is where you will use the fibers you have on-hand. You will be creating your first Bargello Chevron design. Put the diamond pattern together in any way that pleases you, or follow my design which appears on the next page.

If you would like to make the next two projects into something more than a small Bargello exercise, here is how to go about expanding Bargello designs. Do not use your doodle canvas. Instead decide on how large you would like your design to be. Pillow sizes range from mini 4" x 4" to the standard 12" x 12" or 14" by 14" square. Or perhaps you would prefer a rectangular pillow; no problem. Cut your 14 count Brown Mono canvas to the proper size. Don't forget the 2" margins on each side. Now find the exact center and mark it with your quilter's pen. Mount the canvas on stretcher bars or on a scroll frame rods and set aside.

Look at Project One on the next page. You have two choices about where to place the exact center. It will be either the center stitch between the middle diamonds, or the center stitch in the middle of a diamond. You will have to work that out according to the size of your project and your preference. Your next choice is whether to keep the space between row one and two, or to have the diamonds touching as they do on the bottom of the project. If you choose the first option you will create a larger diamond motif with a new secondary design line. This is a perfect choice if you wish to use two contrasting color families. You will have to figure out your own coloring method and that should be fun. If you do not wish to use all the variations in shading, just choose the ones you like. You may also alternate them line by line. This is how you will eventually use all the design lines provided in this book. By changing what you wish, and keeping what you like, you will make the design an expression of your own creativity.

**Please Note: Most of the charts in this book have been enlarged or stretched to make them easier to follow. Check the dimensions on each project, and see the finished work in the color section.**

# PROJECT ONE
## *Shaded Chevron Diamonds*

The diamonds in the first row are all different. The second row illustrates the same shading principals in opposing diamonds. The last section is an overall color pattern of chevron diamonds.

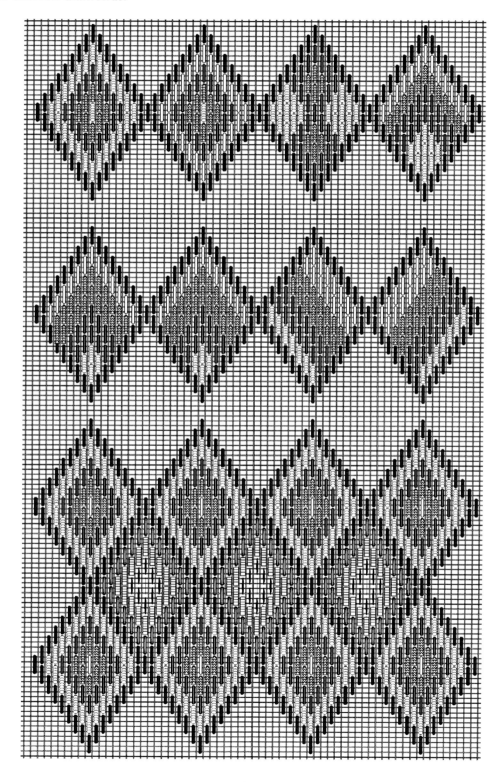

# PROJECT TWO
## *Shading the Bargello Arch*

This is the first time I have presented you with a squared off design. When you fit a design into a given area you will always have to employ compensation stitches. In this case, they are the small stitches covering two threads at the top and the bottom of each section. There are also compensation stitches in the center oval in the second section. These examples are three of the ways that you can design with the lovely Bargello arch. You will find many others as you journey through the four teaching samplers that follow this exercise.

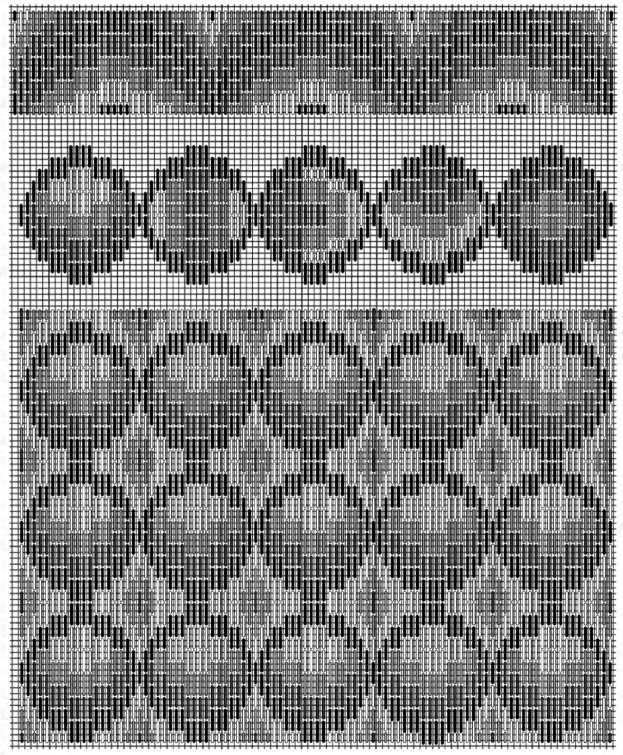

Now that you have done a little shading, let's go back to those samples that you stitched in the preceding chapter. Color them in with your threads in a way that pleases you. Remember the principals of color we discussed at the beginning of this chapter. If you shade a chevron diamond in contrasting colors that are opposite each other on the color wheel or in black and white, that diamond will vibrate and practically jump off of your canvas. If you choose to use only reds, yellow and oranges, you will have a canvas that is sunny, warm and cheerful. If you choose blues, violets and greens, your canvas will be cool and restful. If you choose to use secondary and tertiary colors such as mauves, blue-grays, or browns (other than Sienna), your canvas will be muted or, in the opinion of some folks, very sophisticated.

The following charts are learning projects. I would hope you will do all of them since each is a different learning experience. I am, however, a realist, so pick your favorites after you have done the first two basic samplers. You will find color pictures of each of the following projects in the color section of the book. Study them before stitching, even if you do change the color selections. You should always feel free to do this.

You may find it helpful to color the graphs using colored pencils. Do not use felt-tip pens or markers as they will bleed through the paper. You might want to copy and enlarge the project graph to make it easier to see the design. When you feel comfortable with Bargello, you might find it easier to follow the designs by working from the colored pictures in the book.

There is a wealth of information in the following projects. The design lines presented are for you to use in many different ways. For instance, the first sampler, *Winter Wonder*©, has four design lines. Each can be expanded to do a whole project on its own. The same is true of each of the first four band samplers. They all contain a number of individual designs which can be expanded into many projects. You will see examples of expanded designs taken from these projects at the end of this chapter.

Your canvas can also evoke the feeling of a season. In the next two learning samplers, you will have a winter chevron sampler and a fall curved sampler to stitch. Winter colors are whites, blues, silver metallic and the sparkling metallic blends. Variegated threads in the proper colors add an interesting touch to any project, especially Bargello projects. Today's sheer polyesters and polymer fibers look just like water, snow or ice. If you use my thread suggestions for the *Winter Wonder*© canvas that follows, you will be using all of these fibers.

Fall colors are greens, orange, red, rust, yellow and gold metallic fibers. In the *Fall Fantasy*© sampler, you will be stitching with all of the canvas colors that I have mentioned above. Red and green with touches of gold is Christmas, just as blue and white with touches of silver denotes Chanukah.

Red, White and Blue are the colors of the USA. On the color pages you will find a patriotic red clutch purse just waiting to go to a Fourth of July picnic. Black, paired with metallic silver or gold, is sophisticated. You wouldn't stitch a little girl's canvas in those colors. You would, however, be right on the mark with white and pink; the colors of innocence. I could go on and on, but I hope I have made my point.

Before we begin stitching, let me explain what we will be trying to achieve in this chapter. The next two canvases are learning samplers for both chevron and curved Bargello elements.

**Projects five and six, *Silk on Satin*© and *Twists and Turns*©,** are full blown, intermediate Bargello band samplers. If you follow my thread suggestions you will work with silk, rayon and other luxurious fibers. These two projects were designed by me for Rainbow Gallery, and they have graciously allowed me to reproduce several of my designs in this book.

Following *Twists and Turns*© you will find **Razzle Dazzle Masked Men**© which is a small project designed to give you experience in coloring a half-dropped design line.

Next you will find **Wings**© which is a first step in free form coloring. The fiber used is Alpaca, in colors that are masculine and perfect for hanging in one's office.

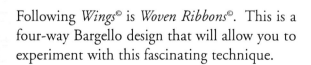

Following *Wings*© is *Woven Ribbons*©. This is a four-way Bargello design that will allow you to experiment with this fascinating technique.

The next project is *Cherries and Pears©*, the cover of this book. In this exercise you will not get a chart, but you will get a template of the design which you can trace onto your canvas. You can use the cover photo as your guide.

The last projects in this chapter are three little fun pieces that I call *Birthday Bargello©*. The design lines are based on birthdates of people special to you. These are exercises in three forms of shading. Look for the pictures in the color section and study the three different ways that a design line can be presented.

You will find more design lines and the projects they were used with in chapter six. This chapter contains advanced designs to stimulate your creativity. Should you stitch all these projects? It depends on how much you enjoy Bargello. If you love it as I do, you will want to learn how to do your own designs.

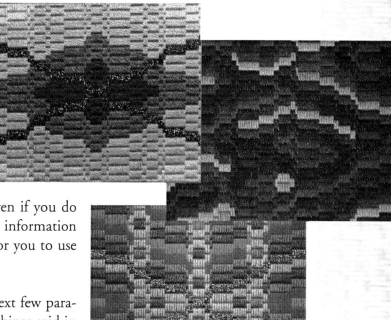

Even if you do not stitch all of the projects, the information contained in them will be there for you to use in all your future designs.

Here are a few words about the next few paragraphs. I will be repeating some things said in Chapter II. I am not writing the following paragraphs just to make the book longer. If you are a needle worker and, at all like me, you may have skimmed through the chapter on getting started. There are some important points concerning Bargello that every one needs to know. Please read the following and save yourself from mistakes later.

It is always wise to practice basic Bargello stitching habits. I call them habits because there really are no rules in needlepoint. However, there are practices that make sense. The length of your thread is one area that is important. As we travel through these pages you will find some beautiful threads used and discussed. Some of these fibers are more fragile than others. If I am using wool or a treated silk, I will experiment with a longer length of thread than usual. If I am stitching with some of the softer wools such as Angora or Alpaca, I would shorten the length of thread used. In every instance you should experiment. Cut a longer thread at first and see how much wear occurs as you stitch. Since you will be working on a frame, (I hope), there will be less wear and tear on the fiber. Another good rule of thumb is to always use a needle threader. Aside from saving you the frustration of threading the needle, a threader will help to preserve the working end of your fiber.

I like to use a number 22 needle when stitching Bargello on 18 count canvas and a number 20 needle on 14 count canvas. I find that Colonial Needle's "Tapestry Petites" are perfect for my hands. They have the same size eyes as regular tapestry needles but are shorter. Because you will be working with many colors, you will find it convenient to have a needle for each color. I thread several needles with each color in my design and keep them ready in my pin cushion. Of course my needle threader and a laying tool are always by my side when I stitch.

You will start your stitching with a waste knot. This is a knot that lies on the top of the canvas and is positioned so that you will stitch over the thread on the back of the canvas. You need do this only at the start of a piece of Bargello. I also mentioned the need for long tails as you start and stop your threads. Bargello stitches are long. Start your thread running away from the place you will begin, and then back again, forming a "J". It is important to trim all loose ends on the back of your canvas. In Bargello, more than other forms of needlepoint, these tails will come to the front of your canvas and are very hard to remove.

Try to stitch your design so that your needle goes into an occupied hole in the canvas. This will lessen the chance of bringing those odd thread tails up into your design. In Bargello stitching you always try for maximum coverage on the rear of your canvas. As you look at the back of a Bargello design, you will see long and short stitches. The long stitches are usually the back of the bundles of stitches like those that form the Bargello arch. The shorter stitches are formed when you travel up and down. Stitching into previous stitches will help you achieve the right stitching tension.

**Remember to constantly check your work!** I cannot stress this enough. A Bargello design gone wrong is impossible to correct in any way other than removing all the stitches back to the error. The designs are so geometrical that mistakes are easy to spot when you make them. Keep checking the tops and the bottoms of the arches, chevrons and medallions as you stitch. The top bundles or stitches and the bottom bundles or stitches should always line up across the canvas.

The more Bargello stitching that you do the more automatic the process becomes. Soon you will notice an error within a few stitches. Please do not think that I am over emphasizing a laborious or difficult task.

I know you will want to see how the colors work together, but please **<u>stitch your design lines first.</u>** It is easy to correct mistakes when only the design line appears on the canvas. Remember, if the design line is wrong, the entire canvas will also be wrong.

The first project is called *Winter Wonder©*. It is an exercise in shading variations of the chevron. *Winter Wonder©* is a band sampler. That is not a musical comment but a description of a sampler that is done in bands. In this sampler there are four bands and each is presented separately. The first band is divided in half. On the left is the moiré shading method and on the right the striped method. The design line is a variegated material. The bottom stitch of the center chevron is where the break occurs. This stitch is located one stitch below the center hole in order to make the design even from top to bottom and from side to side.

The second band is an exercise in shading diamonds. The design line is white and the background has a faintly contrasting beige color next to the white followed by more white. Why did I do this? The projects' intent is to invoke winter weather. The variegated design line in the first band, and the white on white background on the second band are meant to suggest first, an icy night and second, a day when the wind is blowing snow around, so that objects appear and disappear as you are viewing the scenery.

The third band is the Hungarian chevron. Pay attention! This is the first time you have stitched the six, six, two, two pattern. The step up and down is only one thread. If you get lost here, trace a vertical line on the chart. You will see that the stitches go up the canvas like this; two stitches over six threads followed by two stitches over two threads. It is not hard to find your place if you do this. All Hungarian patterns have some variation of this vertical progression. This band is colored to represent a starry, sparkly night in winter.

The fourth band is a diagonal chevron. The pattern represents icicles hanging from roof tops. Look in the color section for figure 11, the small dragon picture (see also at right). I used a variation of this pattern to form a border at the top and bottom of the dragon.

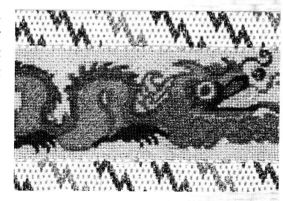

# PROJECT THREE
## *Winter Wonder*
### *COLOR FIGURE 1*

The finished sampler is 5" x 11 1/2". Cut 14 count Mono canvas to 9" x 15". Use masking tape on the raw edges of the canvas and attach to stretcher bars or scroll frame rods. You will need embroidery scissors, size 20 or 22 needles, a needle threader and a laying tool.

**The fibers used in *Winter Wonder*<sup></sup>.**

The fibers used in *Winter Wonder*©.
These fibers come from Rainbow Gallery and are wound on cards. You will need one card of each color.

Band One
    Design line shown in **black**-Overture®, V70-Sky
    Line shown in **white**-Neon Rays®, N55-True Blue
    Line shown **in light gray**-Petite Frosty Rays®, PY040-Medium Blue Gloss
    Line shown **in dark gray**-Very Velvet™, V259-Pale Blue

Band Two
    Design line in **white**-Very Velvet™, V202-White
    Line around diamonds shown in **white triangles**-Very Velvet™, V203-Ecru
    Lightest Blue shown in **white squares**-Very Velvet™, V259-Pale Blue
    Light Blue shown in **light gray**-Very Velvet™, V241-Lite Antique Blue
    Middle Blue shown in **white circles**-Very Velvet™, V218-Antique Blue
    White Iridescent shown in **white triangles**- Razzle-Dazzle 6, D307-White Pearl
    Dark Blue shown in **dark gray**-Very Velvet™, V219-Denim
    Darkest Blue shown in **black**-Very Velvet™, V230-Navy

Band Three
    Design Line shown in **black**-Razzle-Dazzle 6, D330-Blue Multi
    Darker Blue shown in **white circles**-Sparkle Rays, SR74-Colonial Blue
    Lighter Blue shown in **dark gray**-Water N' Ice, WT2-Water Blue
    White Iridescent shown in **white triangles**- Razzle-Dazzle 6, D307-White Pearl
    White Background shown in **white**-Very Velvet™, V202-White

Band Four
    Design Line shown in **black**-Razzle-Dazzle 6, D330-Blue Multi
    Blue shown in **white circles**-Neon Rays®, N55-True Blue
    Lighter Blue in **light gray**-Petite Frosty Rays®, PY040-Medium Blue Gloss
    Lightest Blue shown in **white boxes**-Water N' Ice, WT2-Water Blue
    Lightest Dark Blue shown in **dark gray**- Sparkle Rays, SR74-Colonial Blue
    Dark Blue shown in **white triangles**-Very Velvet™, V219-Denim
    Darkest Blue shown in **black**-Very Velvet™, V230-Navy

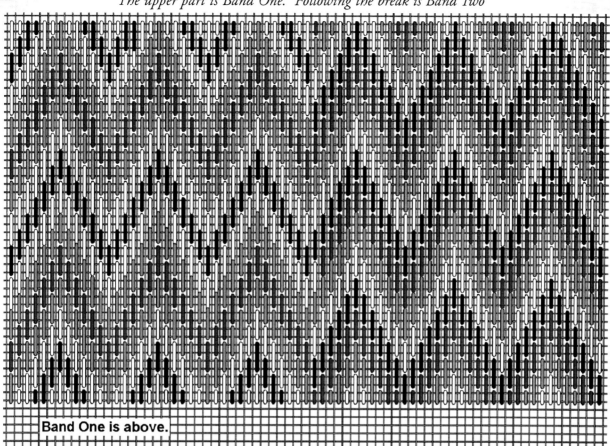

**Band One is above.**

**Band Two is below**

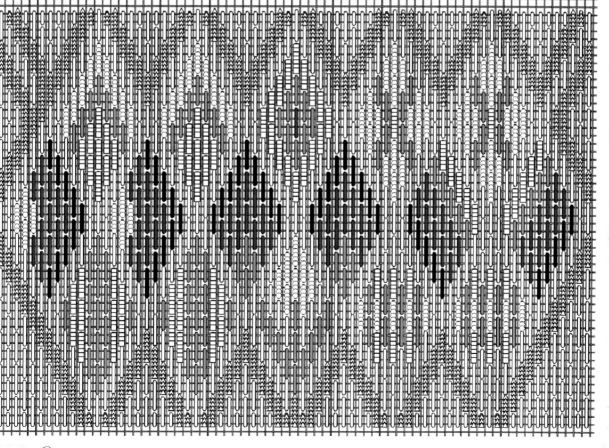

On chart below, Band Three is on top and band Four is after the break.

Band Three

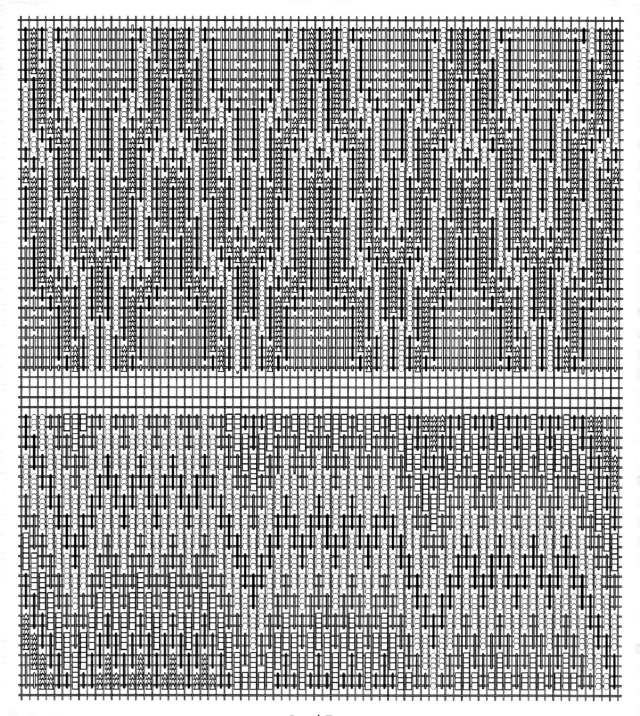

Band Four

# PROJECT FOUR
## *Fall Fantasy*©
### COLOR FIGURE 5

Even though this project is called Fall Fantasy©, I would point out that if you switched the colors used here with those we just used, winter would become fall and vice versa. So you see, the design line may set the pattern but it is the colors that make the design. *Fall Fantasy*© is also a band sampler. In this case there are five bands. The finished sampler is 5" x 9". Cut your 14 count brown Mono canvas to 9" x 13" and attach to stretcher bars or the rods of a rolling frame. Cover the raw edges of the canvas with masking tape. You will need embroidery scissors, size 20 or 22 needles, a needle threader and a tool for laying threads.

These fibers come from Rainbow Gallery and are wound on cards. You will need one card of each color.

The fibers used in Fall Fantasy:
Band One
　　Upper Woven Ribbon in **thin black line**-Rainbow Tweed, RT63-Autumn
　　Lower Woven Ribbon Line in **heavy black line**-Rainbow Tweed, RT65-Deep Green
　　Darkest Red shown in **heavy dark gray line**-Frosty Rays®, Y318-Midnight Red Gloss
　　Middle Red shown in **heavy gray line**-Frosty Rays®, Y072-Dark Red Gloss
　　Lightest Red shown in **gray ellipse**-Flair®, F529-Dark Red
　　Brown Background shown in **white**-Flair®, F554-Golden Brown
Band Two
　　Design Line shown in **heavy black line**-Rainbow Tweed, RT65-Deep Green
　　Brown shown in **heavy white line**-Flair®, F554-Golden Brown
　　Lighter Brown shown in **white circles**-Frosty Rays®, Y347-Goldenrod Gloss
　　Gold shown in **dark gray ellipse**-Sparkle Rays, SR53-Dark Marigold
Band Three
　　Design Line shown in **thin black line**-Rainbow Tweed, RT63-Autumn
　　Green shown in **heavy black line**-Rainbow Tweed, RT65-Deep Green
　　Brown shown in **heavy white line**-Flair®, F554-Golden Brown
　　Lighter Brown shown in **white circles**-Frosty Rays®, Y347-Goldenrod Gloss
　　Gold shown in **dark gray ellipse**-Sparkle Rays, SR53-Dark Marigold
Band Four is the same color as band two, only reversed.
Band Five is the same color as band one, only reversed.
The complete chart is on the next page.

This design would make a great Christmas canvas. Substitute the gold Flair for a brown metallic fiber. Expand the design horizontally for a place mat and make matching napkin rings out of band two. If you have guests coming and own a luggage rack, expand band one to fit the rack and choose colors that match your guest room.

The point that I am making is that Bargello is a very useful skill. It is quick and easy, fun to do, and adaptable to many uses. Use the designs in this book as whole entities, or borrow an element to make whatever you desire. Your local needlepoint shop will be happy to help you plan projects. They may even have templates for check book covers, tissue boxes and other useful gift items.

The chart below is made up of five separate bands. The borders of each band are easy to find. Just look for the small compensation stitches that run over two threads. The bands are numbered on the right hand border of the chart.

*Fall Fantasy*©

# Silk on Satin©

## COLOR FIGURE 6

Design Size: 4 1/2" x 13"

Cut 18 count white Mono Canvas 10" x 17". All fibers are by Rainbow Gallery. You need one card of each color with the exception of Patina which requires two cards. Begin 4 1/2" down and 3" in from the left side. Use #20 tapestry needles.

Splendor®-S832- Dark Green
Silk & Cream-BG23-Sky Blue
Silk & Cream-BG2-Silk and Cream
Silk & Cream-BG21-Champagne
Gold Rush 14™-WG4C-Arctic Gold
Gold Rush 14™-WG35C-White Gold
Patina®-PA255-Lite Taupe Gray

Use eight plies of Splendor. You must separate the plies of silk. It is easy to do this if you hold it in the same direction that it comes off the card when you cut. Pull out one strand of silk; it will slip out smoothly. Your stitches will look their best if you use a laying tool when stitching with Splendor Silk. Use all other fibers as they come off the card. Try breaking the Gold Rush 14 fiber instead of cutting. Breaking chainette threads locks the chain and there is less chance of it raveling. The color key and band one is below.

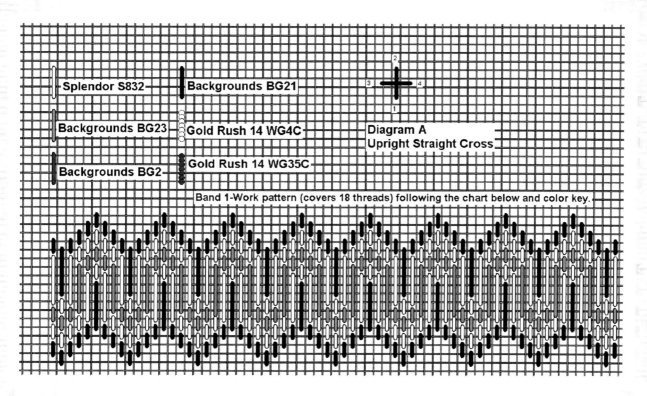

Leave eight canvas threads open between the lowest point of Band One and the start of Band Two.

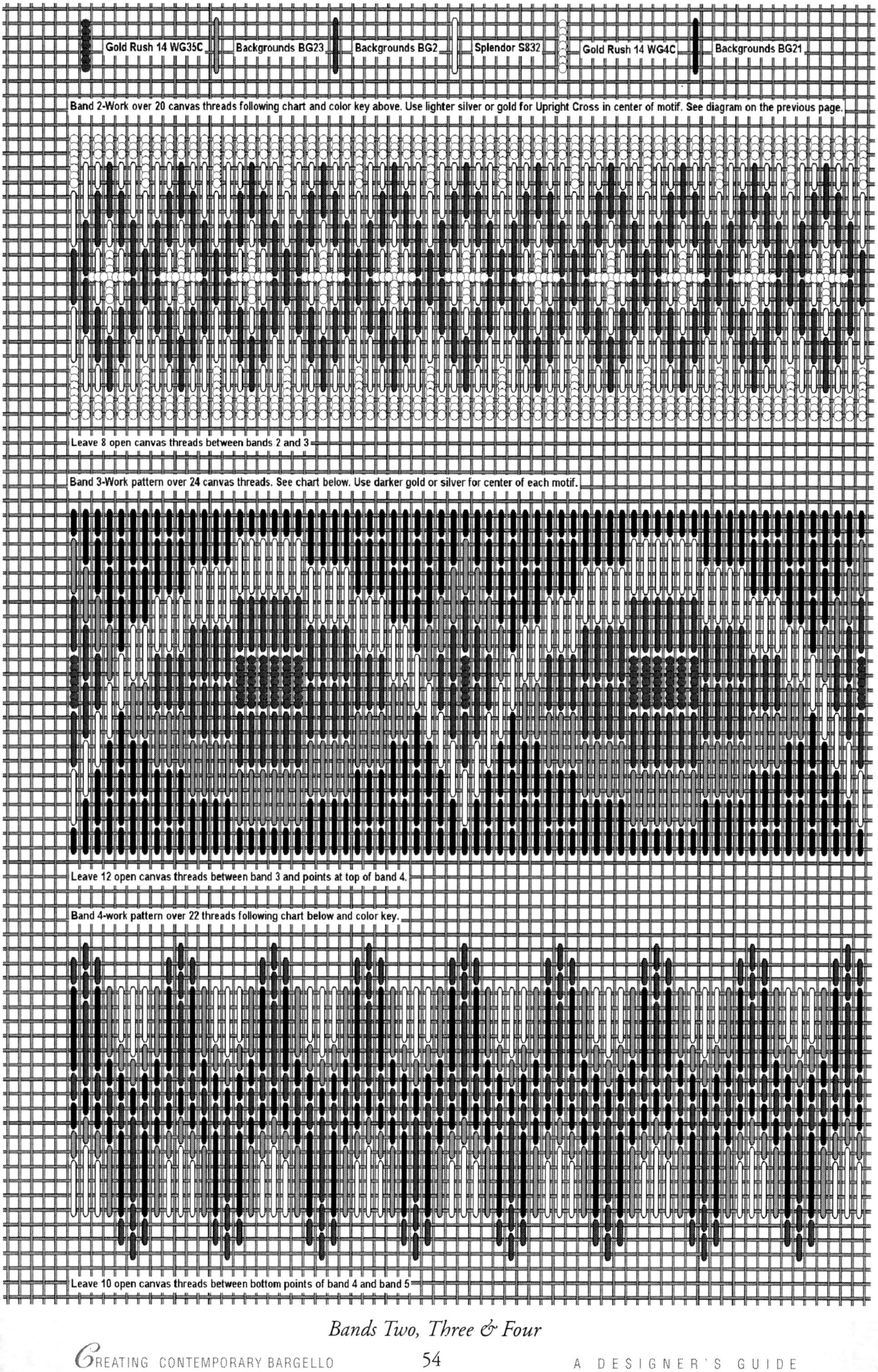

Gold Rush 14 WG35C | Backgrounds BG23 | Backgrounds BG2 | Splendor S832 | Gold Rush 14 WG4C | Backgrounds BG21

Band 2-Work over 20 canvas threads following chart and color key above. Use lighter silver or gold for Upright Cross in center of motif. See diagram on the previous page.

Leave 8 open canvas threads between bands 2 and 3

Band 3-Work pattern over 24 canvas threads. See chart below. Use darker gold or silver for center of each motif.

Leave 12 open canvas threads between band 3 and points at top of band 4.

Band 4-work pattern over 22 threads following chart below and color key.

Leave 10 open canvas threads between bottom points of band 4 and band 5

*Bands Two, Three & Four*

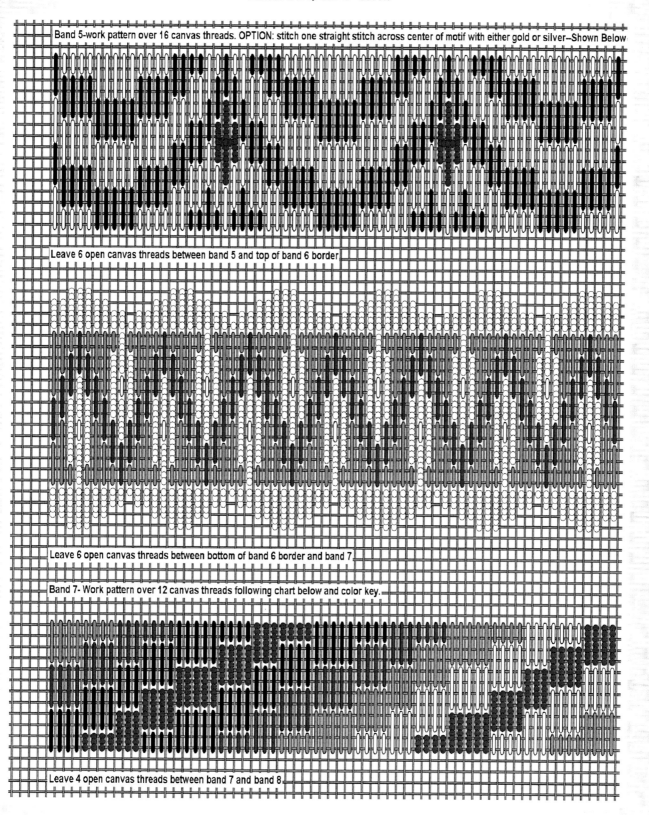

Band 5-work pattern over 16 canvas threads. OPTION: stitch one straight stitch across center of motif with either gold or silver—Shown Below

Leave 6 open canvas threads between band 5 and top of band 6 border

Leave 6 open canvas threads between bottom of band 6 border and band 7

Band 7- Work pattern over 12 canvas threads following chart below and color key.

Leave 4 open canvas threads between band 7 and band 8

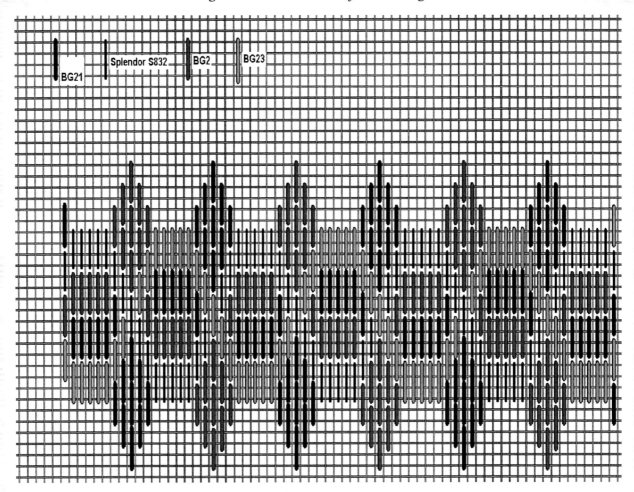

BG21    Splendor S832    BG2    BG23

**BACKGROUND**— Fill in background with Web Stitch starting 10 open threads above the points of Band 1. Use Patina (PA21-Lite Taupe Gray). See Diagram B for count and Diagram C for compensation around points of Band 1. Place Web Stitch in balance of background areas compensating when necessary. Add background to cover 10 threads **below** points of Band 8. Work 2 vertical rows of Slanted Gobelin (over 2 threads) down each side of design using Patina. See photograph and Diagram D.

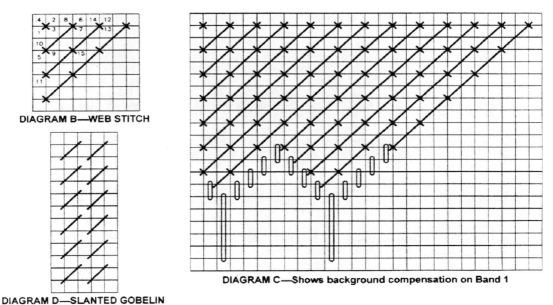

DIAGRAM B—WEB STITCH

DIAGRAM C—Shows background compensation on Band 1

DIAGRAM D—SLANTED GOBELIN

# PROJECT SIX
## *Twists and Turns*©
### *COLOR FIGURE 10*

Design Size: 5 1/2"x 13 1/2". Cut 18 count white Mono Canvas 10" x 18". Use #20 tapestry needle, scroll frame, laying tool and needle threader.

All fibers are from Rainbow Gallery. You will need one card of each of the following:

Splendor®-S836-Dark Forest Green       Gold Rush 14™-WG27C-Vatican Gold
Splendor®-S831-Forest Green            Super Suede-SS41-Champagne
Splendor®-S837-Sea Green               Super Suede-SS46-Spice
Splendor®-S852-Very Dark Brown         Super Suede-SS47-Dark Brown
Splendor®-S844-Dark Fawn               Patina®-PA253-Sage
Splendor®-S843-Fawn                    Frosty Rays®-Y209-Multi Blue Ice
Splendor®-S896-Very Dark Flesh 1       Arctic Rays-AR3-Ecru
Splendor®-S895-Dark Flesh              Rainbow Angora-RA03-Ecru
Splendor®-S894-Medium Flesh            Backgrounds-BG6-Helene-Natural
Gold Rush 14™-WG9C-Bronze              Silk & Cream-BG32-Pale Peach
Gold Rush 14™-J51C-Brown

Use eight plies of Splendor. You must separate the plies of silk. It is easy to do this if you hold it in the same direction that it comes off the card when you cut. Pull out one strand of silk; it will slip out smoothly. Your stitches will look their best if you use a laying tool when stitching with Splendor Silk. Use all other fibers as they come off the card. Try breaking the Gold Rush 14 fiber instead of cutting. Breaking chainette threads locks the chain and there is less chance of it raveling.

Each band has its own color key. Because there is such a variety of fibers, I had to use the same symbols for several fibers. Follow the individual color keys as they appear on each band. Attach canvas to stretcher bars or scroll rods. Measure down two inches from the top of the canvas, and two inches in from the left side. This will be the top left corner of the border. Follow the pattern and border legend of band one chart.

Use one strand of Gold Rush 14 and 6 ply of Splendor. The background Web Stitch uses four ply of Splendor. See diagram for count of Web Stitch. Placement is shown on band one chart. Work the balance of the border in web stitch background as you continue down the band charts. Note the border compensations on sides of band four.

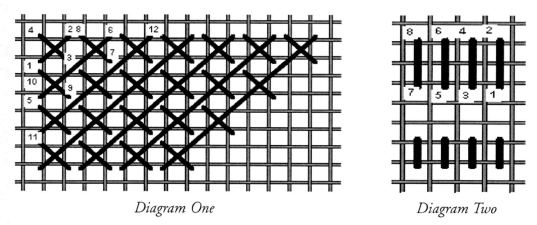

*Diagram One*          *Diagram Two*

**Band One**-Work pattern over 23 threads following band one chart and legend for color. There is a band of Gobelin stitches over three threads at the top of the pattern and over two threads at the bottom. See diagram two for count. Use Patina as it comes off the card. Take the kink out of the thread by moistening it. Use six ply of Splendor, and one each of the metallics. Super Suede is used as it comes off the card. This fiber does not look good if twisted. Use your laying tool. The same applies to Splendor. Silk reflects the light best when the strands lie evenly next to each other. This is especially true in Bargello.

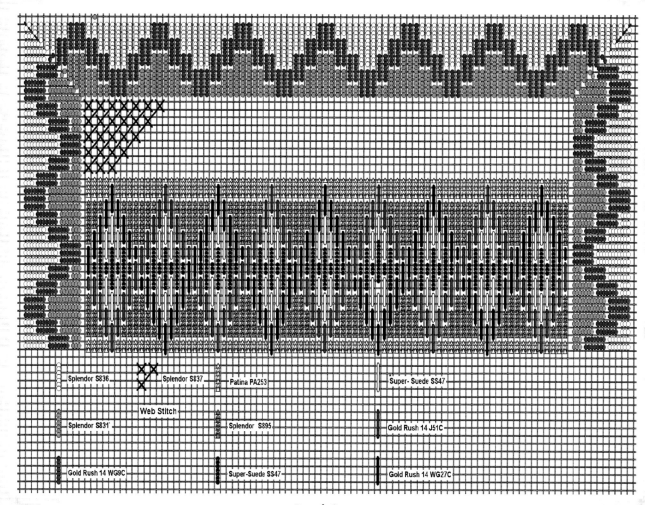

*Band One*

**Band Two**-This two-color design is stitched over 22 threads with 6 ply of Splendor and 1 strand of Artic Rays. Use a needle threader with the Artic Rays, and stitch this fiber after the Splendor silk so that the fuzzy fringe does not get pulled down. Follow band 2 chart and color legend which is below.

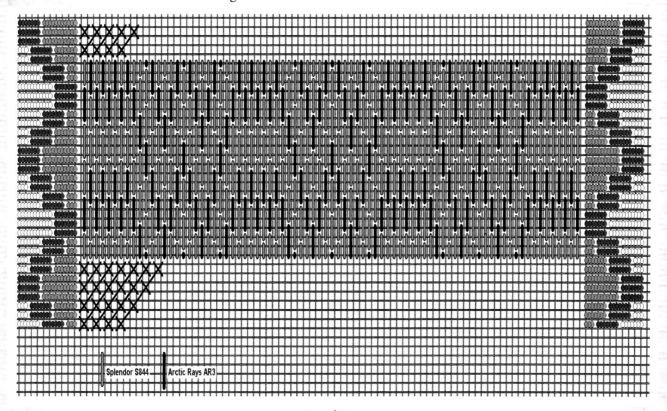

*Band Two*

*Diagram Three*

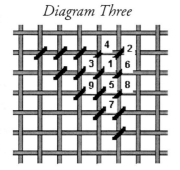

**Band Three**-Work pattern over 28 threads following band 3 chart and color legend. It is easiest to start at either the right or left side of the pattern. Begin with one strand of Silk & Cream. Stitch the first design line up to the single stitch of Frosty Rays. Continue to fill in this section with 6 ply each of Splendor S895 and S896. When you have done this, fill in the Frosty Rays design line using 1 strand. You will find that this nylon tubing is easier to stitch with if you cut it at an angle. The Basketweave background fills in between the upper and lower Web Stitch background. See diagram three. Use 1 strand of Patina for the Basketweave. You may have heard that rayon threads, such as Patina, are difficult to stitch with. You will find this fiber delightful as long as you remember to moisten it to remove the kinks and to use a needle threader. The other important thing to remember about rayon is that it is slippery and needs to be well anchored. When you begin a thread on the back of the canvas, pull the thread away from your starting point and then back to it forming a "J". Do this when you end the thread as well. Note that there are some compensation stitches on the side center motifs. The chart is not wrong, but if the uneven Basketweave blocks are displeasing to you, allow the small amount of canvas to show at the sides.

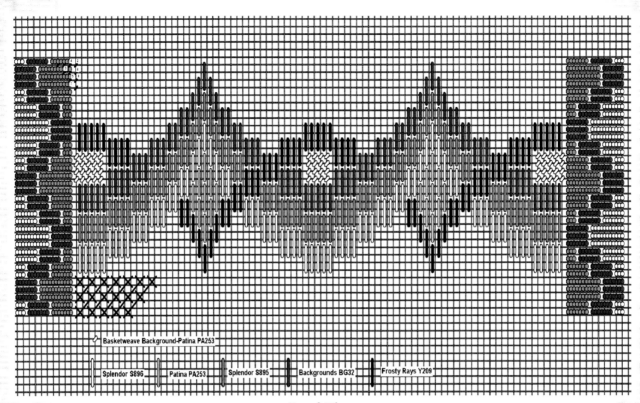

*Band Three*

*Diagram Four*

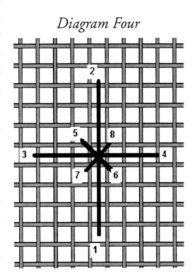

**Band Four**-Work pattern over 32 threads following band four chart and color legend. This band is an adaptation of a four-way Bargello design. Study the chart before you begin to stitch. Starting in the center, lay in the motifs first. You will notice that the stitches run either over 4 or 2 canvas threads with a step up or down of one canvas thread. This is typical of Hungarian Point Bargello. See Diagram Four on the previous page for the center star. The background is stitched with one strand of Backgrounds BG6. Do not use too long of a strand as you will want to maintain the soft lustrous look of this lovely fiber.

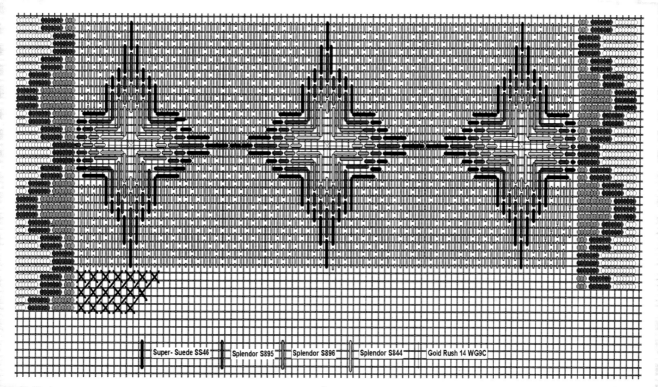

*Band Four*

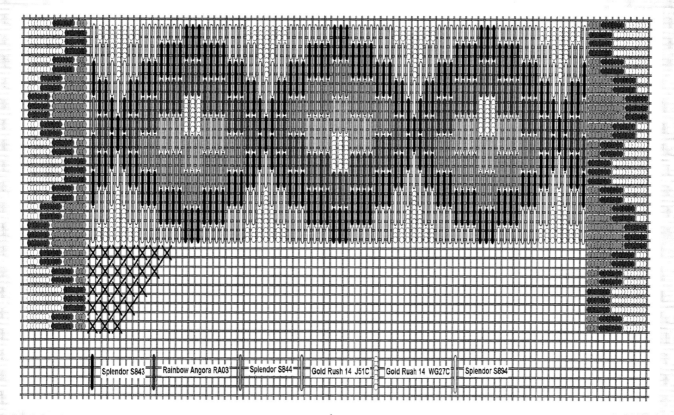

*Band Five*

**Band Five**-This traditional Bargello is stitched over 24 threads. Be careful with the angora thread. Use short strands and a needle threader. Move your needle often while stitching so that the thread will not be stressed at one point. Stitch the Angora last so that the soft furry texture is shown to its best advantage.

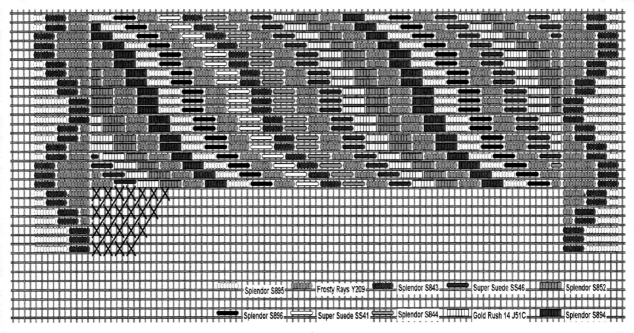

Splendor S895    Frosty Rays Y209    Splendor S843    Super Suede SS46    Splendor S852

Splendor S896    Super Suede SS41    Splendor S844    Gold Rush 14 J51C    Splendor S894

*Band Six*

**Band Six**-This band is stitched into **19 spaces** of the canvas. See band 6 chart. You will see that the stitches run horizontally. This is what creates the wavy ribbon effect and is one of the "twists" referred to in the title of this project. Use your laying tool when working this band.

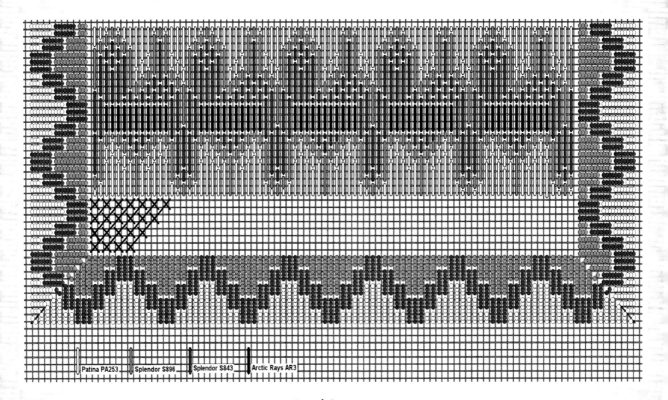

Patina PA253    Splendor S896    Splendor S843    Arctic Rays AR3

*Band Seven*

**Band Seven**-Work pattern over 24 threads following the chart. Stitch the Splendor first, then the Artic Rays. The background is stitched with a single strand of Patina. You will be following a Hungarian Point pattern covering either 6 or 2 threads, and moving up and down in steps of one.

# *Razzle-Dazzle 6 Masked Men*©

## *COLOR FIGURE 20*

The finished canvas is 8" x 7 1/2". Cut your 14 count brown Mono canvas to 12" x 12" and attach to stretcher bars or the rods of a scroll frame. Cover the raw edges of the canvas with masking tape. You will need embroidery scissors, size 20 or 22 needles, a needle threader and a tool for laying threads.

*Fibers for Razzle-Dazzle 6 Masked Men*©

These fibers come from Rainbow Gallery and are wound on cards. You will need one card of each color.

The Following colors are Frosty Rays®:
  Shown as a **thick white line**-Y209-Multi Blue Ice
  Shown as a **thick black line**-Y023-Dark Waters
  Shown as **thin black line**-Y030-Pale Antique Blue Gloss
  Shown as **thin black ellipse**-Y032-Light Antique Blue Gloss

The Following colors are Razzle-Dazzle 6™
  Shown as **thin dark gray line**-D314-Sky Blue
  Shown as a **thick gray line**-D312-Blue
  Shown as a **thin gray line**-D315-Dark Peacock
  Shown as a **dark gray ellipse**-D328 Pink/Blue/Gold
  Shown as **squares**-D330-Blue Multi
  Shown as **heavy black ellipse**-D329-Black Multi
  Shown as a **thick dark gray line**-D305-Bronze
  Shown as **a striped line**-D304-Silver
  Shown as a **white ellipse**-D302-White Gold
  Shown as **triangles**-D303-Pale Gold

Fyre Werks®
  Shown as a **thin white line**-F9-Copper

This is a half-dropped design with a lot of color changes. The design lines are all in black lines: thick, thin and ellipses. You can find them easily by noting the large diamonds in the center of the design. STITCH ALL OF THE DESIGN LINES FIRST. I admit that this is a complicated design when it comes to the colors, but the overall effect is worth the effort. If you stitch this, I can promise you that you won't find *Razzle-Dazzle 6 Masked Men* anywhere else. By the way, I named the project masked men because that's what the blue sections in the center look like to me. Razzle-Dazzle 6 comes in gold, silver, and copper in several shades. This is good to know, especially when doing holiday canvases which often feature metal objects. If you want to change the colors that I have used, study the colored picture first. Make a list of what goes where and begin by stitching the new design line colors.

The chart is below and the color picture can be found in the color section of the book.

*Razzle-Dazzle 6 Masked Men©*

# PROJECT EIGHT
## *Wings*©
### *COLOR FIGURE 26*

The finished canvas is 9 1/2" x 5 1/2". Cut your 14 count brown Mono canvas to 14" x 10" and attach to stretcher bars or the rods of a scroll frame. Cover the raw edges of the canvas with masking tape. You will need embroidery scissors, size 20 or 22 needles, a needle threader and a tool for laying threads.

Fibers for *Wings*©:

Fibers are from Rainbow Gallery and are wound on cards.

Alpaca 18-AL64 Black-2 cards
Balance of fibers, one card each:
    AL63-Charcoal Gray
    AL62-Dark Gray
    AL61-Gray
    AL58-Dark Cocoa
    AL56-Cocoa #1
    AL55-Light Cocoa
    AL54-Beige
    AL53-Ivory
    AL52-Off White

Cresta d'Oro® (use two strands in your needle):
    C03-Black Gold
    C02-Antique Gold
    C09-Black Silver
    C08-Steel Gray

*Wings*© is a true Free Form Bargello. There is no other design exactly like this anywhere. It begins with a design line repeated from left to right up the canvas. The line gently curves since I have chosen to repeat similar numbers in sequence. The chart is of the design lines only. Even though these lines change their direction, they still maintain the vertical count of the original design line. Remember, any direction and spacing is correct as long as each new line echos that portion of the design line directly below or above it. Stitch all design lines first. Now is your chance to really spread your wings by filling in the colors as you may choose. The charted design lines are on the next page.

Look at the color picture in the color section and notice how I have used the colors listed above.

Just a few words about Cresta d'Oro. This thread is unusual because it comes in a wide variety of shading metallic colors. There are many silver, gold and copper colors in both bright and matte finish you may use to enhance the shading in your needlework designs.

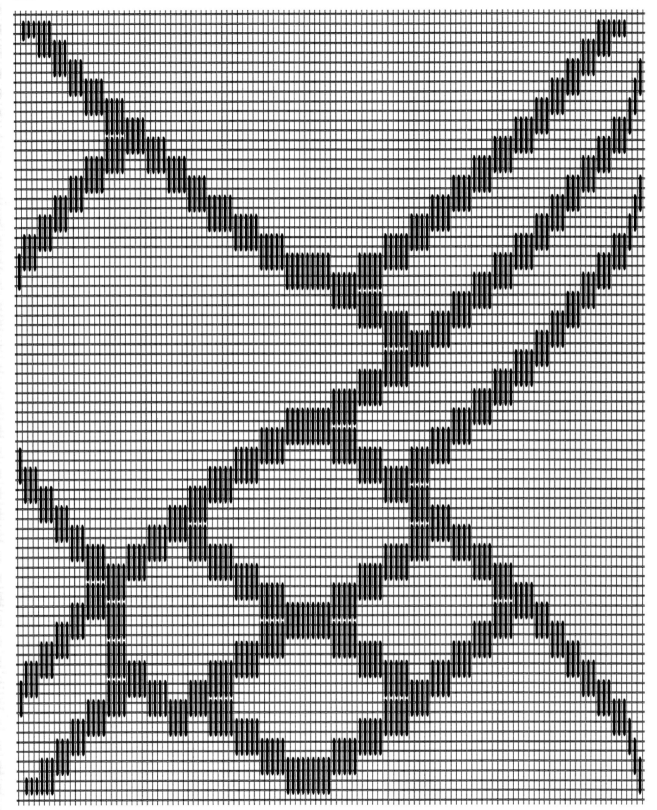

*Wings Design Line*

# *Woven Ribbons©-Four-Way Bargello*

## *COLOR FIGURE 4*

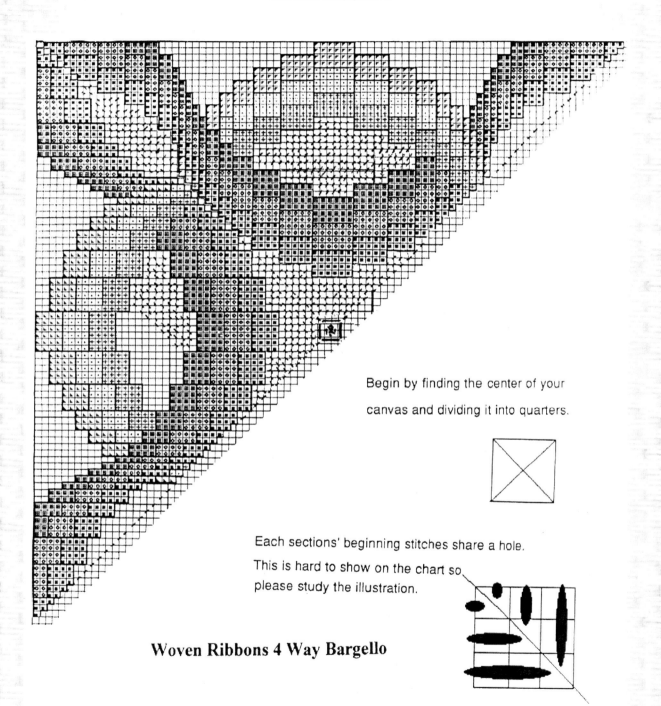

Begin by finding the center of your

canvas and dividing it into quarters.

Each sections' beginning stitches share a hole.

This is hard to show on the chart so

please study the illustration.

### **Woven Ribbons 4 Way Bargello**

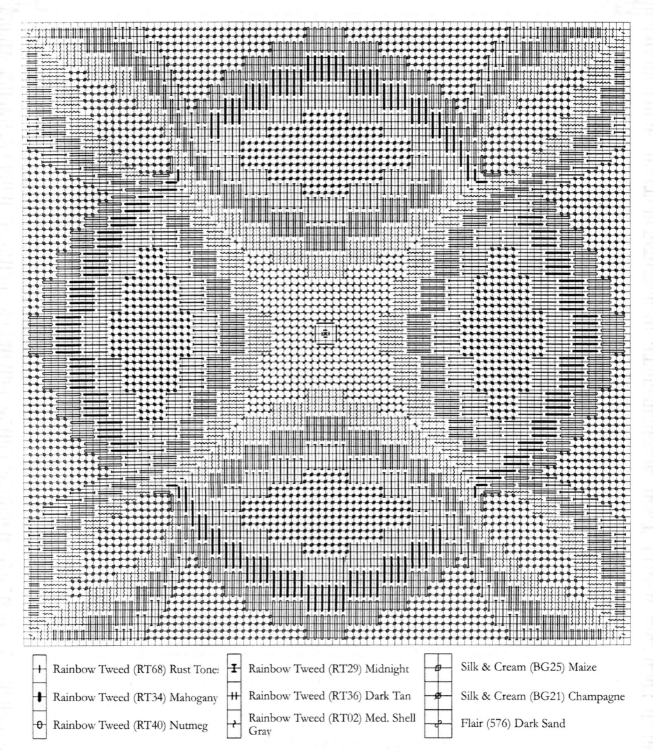

| | | |
|---|---|---|
| ┼ Rainbow Tweed (RT68) Rust Tone | I Rainbow Tweed (RT29) Midnight | ⊞ Silk & Cream (BG25) Maize |
| ┃ Rainbow Tweed (RT34) Mahogany | ╫ Rainbow Tweed (RT36) Dark Tan | ∅ Silk & Cream (BG21) Champagne |
| 0 Rainbow Tweed (RT40) Nutmeg | ⌐ Rainbow Tweed (RT02) Med. Shell Gray | ⊐ Flair (576) Dark Sand |

Finished size: 6"x 6". Canvas size: 11"x11". 14 Count Brown Bargello Canvas, No. 18 tapestry needle. One card each of above colors. Mount canvas on stretcher bars. Mark top. Find center and baste diagonal lines (over 5, under 5) through the center to divide canvas into quarters. Rotate canvas while stitching so that each of the 4 sections is facing you. Center motif is RT68.

# PROJECT TEN
## *Cherries and Pears*©
### THE COVER DESIGN

The finished canvas is 9 1/2" x 9 1/4 ". Cut your 18 count brown Mono canvas to 14" x 14" and attach to stretcher bars or the rods of a scroll frame. Cover the raw edges of the canvas with masking tape. You will need embroidery scissors, size 20 or 22 needles, a needle threader and a laying tool.

I think it would be interesting for you to look at what was going on inside my brain when I was styling *Cherries and Pears©*. Since this would be the cover of my book, I wanted the design to tell as much as possible about what you would find inside.

Chapter Three will give you a variety of stitches that complement Bargello designs. I have used almost all of these stitches in the leaves of the fruit and the background. I chose the glistening nylon ribbon threads from Rainbow Gallery. The Pear is stitched with Flair and Frosty Rays. The Cherries are stitched with Sparkle Rays. The Cherry leaves are also stitched with Sparkle Rays and the stitch used is the Hungarian Ground. The leaves of the pears are stitched with Very Velvet. I chose a less reflective fiber because these leaves lie behind the Pears and the Cherries.

The three Cherries illustrate three types of shading. The top Cherry employs a traditional Bargello shading scheme. The Cherry on the lower right is a more modern style. I chose this so that the Cherry would reflect light from the front. The last Cherry is shaded in a free form style and reflects light from the right side. The leaf behind the Cherry is worked in Brick Stitch.

The Pear on the right is stitched in a traditional Florentine pattern. The leaves are stitched in Very Velvet. The Pavillion Stitch is used for the lighter leaf, and the Hungarian Stitch for the darker leaf. The second Pear is stitched in a traditional lacy Hungarian pattern. The dark leaf is stitched with Very Velvet using the Old Florentine stitch. The lighter leaf in Very Velvet is worked using the Gobelin Stitch. The background is stitched in Silk and Cream which is a blend of silk and wool. I used the Horizontal Brick Stitch over eight threads of canvas.

I have provided you with a template of *Cherries and Pears* on the next page. Copy the template and use it to trace the design on a blank piece of 18 count brown Mono canvas. Use the quilter's pen I mentioned in Chapter One. Tape your template to a window or glass door and place the canvas over it. The outside light will make it easy for you to trace the design. Use the color picture on the cover as your guide. Pick the fibers and colors that appeal to you, keeping in mind the shading and coloring of what you are stitching. You may use the design lines on the cover or any of the design lines in the book. The fibers I selected for *Cherries & Pears* are listed on the page following the template.

*Template for Cherries and Pears*©

**Material list used for the cover design of Cherries and Pears© available from Rainbow Gallery.**

3 cards-Silk and Cream-BG34
1 card each:

    Flair®-F525-Pale Peach
    Flair®-F506-Rose Pink
    Flair®-F526-Dark Peach
    Flair®-F530-Christmas Red
    Flair®-F596-Lite Fawn
    Flair®-F597-Fawn
    Flair®-F504-True Ecru
    Flair®-F503-Ecru
    Flair®-F551-Lite Tan
    Flair®-F553-Old Gold

    Petite Frosty Rays®-PY151-Lite Tan Pearl
    Petite Frosty Rays®-PY062-Golden Tan Gloss
    Petite Frosty Rays®-PY064-Copper Gloss

    Frosty Rays®-Y097-Brown Sparkle Gloss #2

    Sparkle Rays-SR25-Sea Green
    Sparkle Rays-SR24-Light Sea Green
    Sparkle Rays-SR33-Peach
    Sparkle Rays-SR34-Dark Peach
    Sparkle Rays-SR29-Christmas Red

    Very Velvet™-V237-Sea Green
    Very Velvet™-V223-Dark Green
    Very Velvet™-V206-Tan

**CHERRIES AND PEARS©**

# PROJECT ELEVEN
## *Birthday Bargello© Variation A*
### *COLOR FIGURE 12*

These are studies of manipulating both the design line and the coloring. The charts for all three versions follow. These little projects with a design line based on someone's birth date are fun to do.

The chart on the next page is based on our youngest daughter's birthday. She was born on May 2, 1962, so we start in the center with a bundle of five stitches for May, the fifth month. The rest of the line follows down in order so that the whole sequence is 5, 2, 1, 9, 6, 2 or her birthday; 5/2/1962.

I cannot give you the size of your personal project as it depends on the count of the special number sequence you are using. Use the graph paper to work out your design line. You will then know the size of brown Mono 14 count canvas you will need to cut.

I used one card or one skein of each of the fibers listed below. You may need to use more or less depending on your personal number sequence.

From Rainbow Gallery:
    Design Line shown as **black**-Hologram Fyre Werks®-FH12-Dark Blue

Vineyard Classic Silk from Wiltex Threads
    Darkest gray shown as **thin dark gray line**-C-108-Granite
    Middle gray shown as **heavy gray line**-C-107-Heron
    Light gray shown as **dark gray circles**-C-105-Paloma
    Lightest gray shown as **white**-C-104-Evening Haze
    White shown as **dark gray triangles**-C-109-Bright White


The three Birthday Bargello charts are different exercises in the manipulation of colors. In the first chart you have the complete design with the colors and their description.

In the second chart you will find the placement of the colors, but I have left the selection of the colors for to you to pick out. You will find my finished piece in the color section, *Color Figure 13.*

In Birthday Bargello, Variation C you will find only the free form design lines. I have left the selection and placement of colors to your own discretion.

The chart for Birthday Bargello Variation A is on the following page.

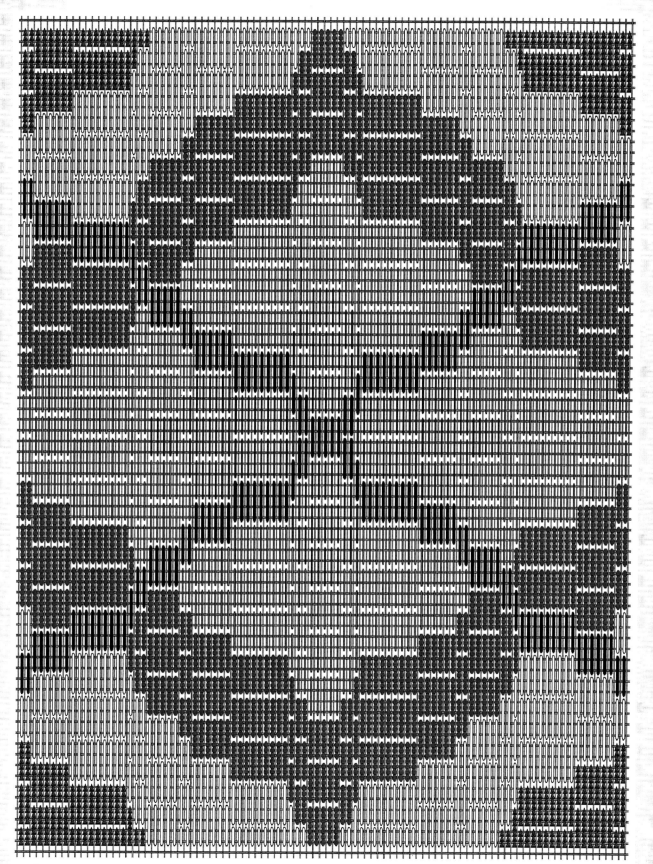

*Birthday Bargello Variation A*

# *Birthday Bargello® Variation* **B**
## *COLOR FIGURE 13*

I was interested in the little medallion pattern formed by the first interpretation. In this design we retain the design line but manipulate the colors in order to create an entirely different look. Below you will find the chart. I used soft beige colors with a gold design line. You can choose any colors that you wish. Just decide what colors in your work basket are represented on the chart and enjoy. The colors of the world are limitless and they all go together nicely.

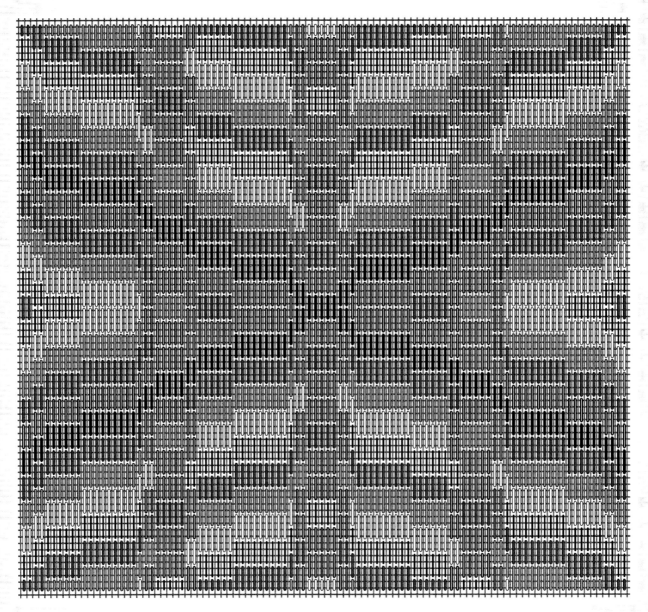

*Birthday Bargello Variation B*

# Birthday Bargello© Variation C
## COLOR FIGURE 14

This design is a free form Bargello pattern. The design line is the same as the previous Birthday Bargello patterns. Here I have broken the line up and allowed it to wander freely over the canvas. This creates interesting little medallions and swirls that you can color in as you please. Look at the pattern below. Notice that the vertical count is always the same. In other words, if there is a bundle of nine on the canvas, all the bundles above and below that bundle will also be bundles of nine. The horizontal pattern of the design line will vary. The vertical pattern never varies. I have not charted the colors of this design for two reasons. First, I want you to get a clear picture of how the design lines travel over the canvas. Second, I thought it would be fun for you to have a coloring book experience. Use any colors you care to and put them any place that pleases you. That is why this is called a free form exercise. Have fun.

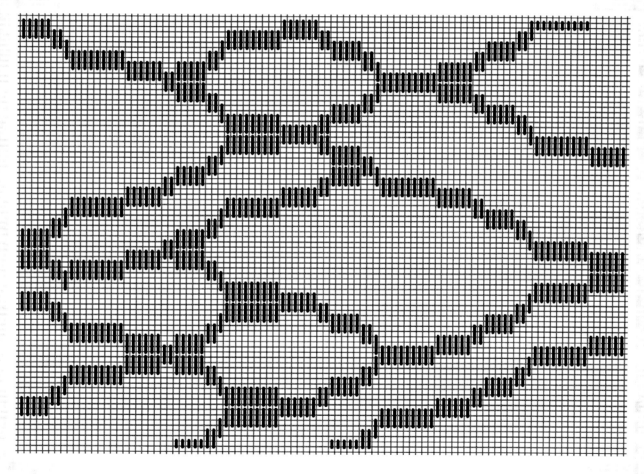

*Birthday Bargello Variation C*

# Expanding Design Lines from the Projects

The following charts are examples of how to expand the designs from the samplers in this book into all-over designs. Use your graph paper and colored pencils to work out your color choices and design line alterations.

*Expanding Band One of Silk on Satin*

On the top version of band two below, I have left the border in as a separate design element.  On the lower version, the border has been removed and the diamonds are touching.

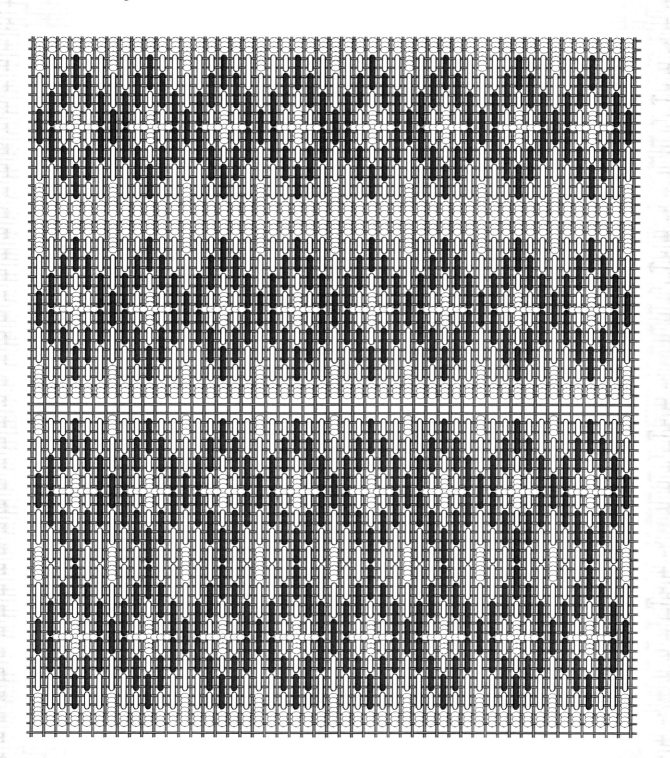

*Expanding Band Five of Silk on Satin*

This is a mirror image version of band five.

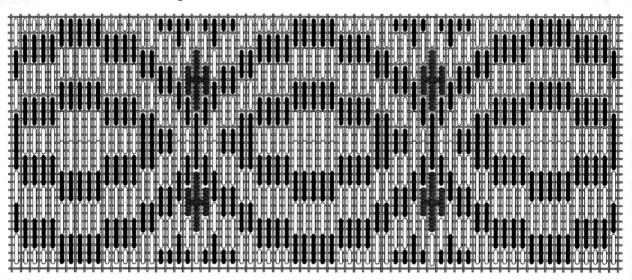

*Expanding Band Four of Twists and Turns*

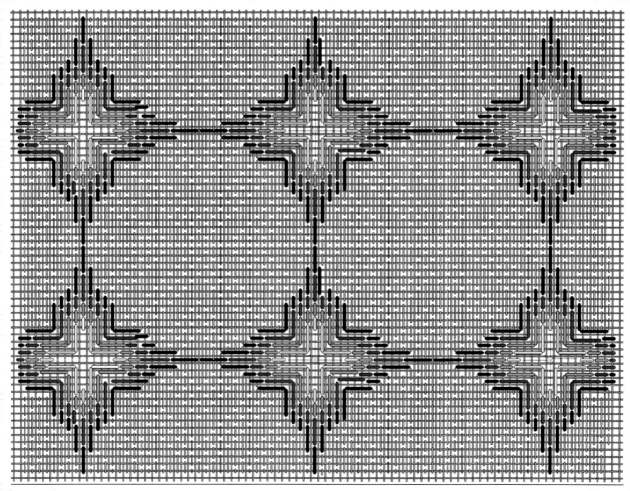

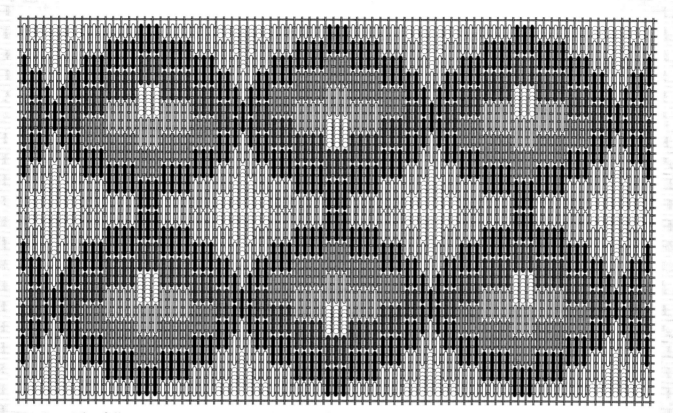

The following pages are manipulations of two design lines that you will find in the projects. The difference here is that the lines have been altered to produce a new effect. If you take a little time with a pencil and some graph paper, you can create wonderful new designs. Make sure that the pencil has a good eraser. It takes a lot of thoughts and decisions to come up with the final design. Another thing I should mention is the fact that manipulated design lines often contain compensating stitches. This is true of the shell pattern I have colored in the second example.

This is the starting point for the first design. The idea is from Band Six of *Twists and Turns*. The line has been rotated from horizontal to vertical and expanded. The results are on the next page.

Before                    After

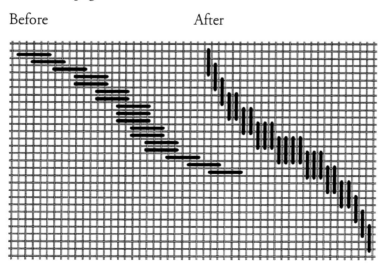

*Expanding a diagonal into a long line*

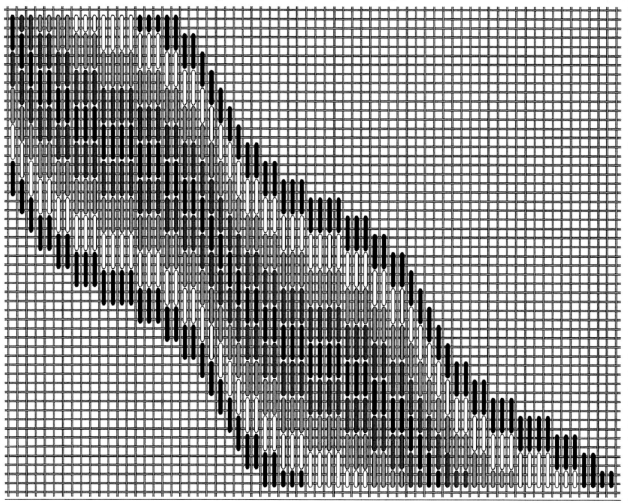

*Expanding diagonal overlay*

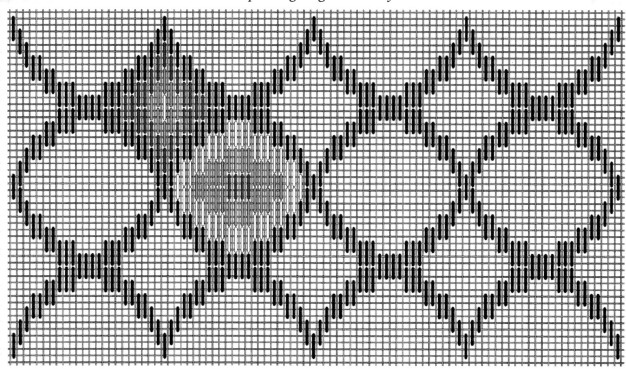

*Expanding joined diagonal lines to form a Pomegranate*

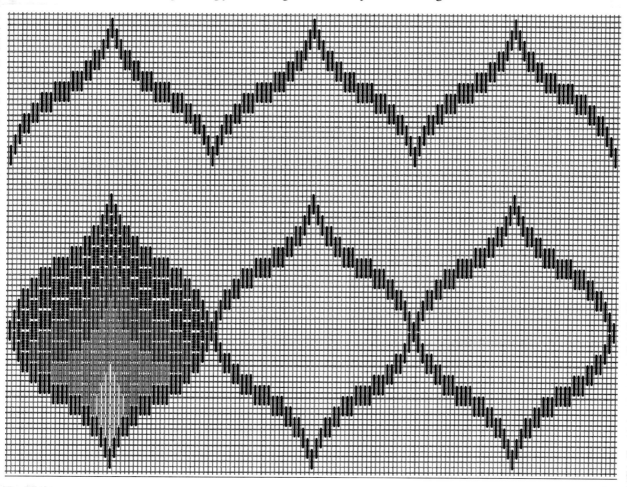

*Expanding the Bargello Arch to form the Scallop or Shell*

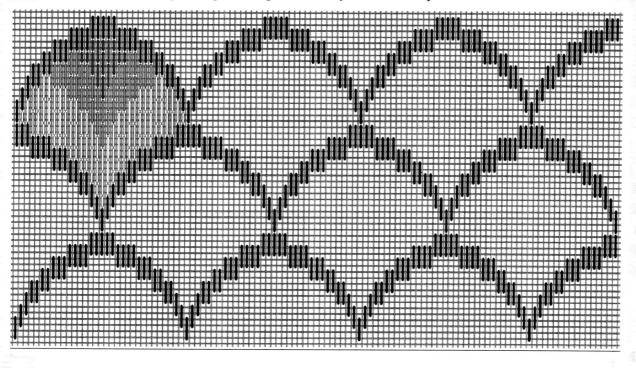

# CHAPTER SIX
## *Projects and Possibilities*

### ADVANCED PROJECTS

The following examples are all mounted on various objects such as chairs, boxes, accessories, and of course pillows. The design lines are here for you to use however you wish. You may expand or reduce any of these designs to fit your special project. I have listed the suppliers of the various items in chapter seven should you desire to stitch them. You may order any of the items shown through your local Needlework shop. If you are unable to locate the item from a local shop, the manufacturer or supplier may be able to advise you where you can obtain it.

### PROJECT TWELVE
## *Bargello Christmas Mini Stocking*
### COLOR FIGURE 21

On the following page you will find project twelve, a Bargello Christmas Mini Stocking and the template for the stocking. Below is the design to be stitched. Here is an idea you might enjoy. Stitch a mini stocking for each guest at your holiday table. Loop a gift tag on each to use as a place card on the dining table. Slip a place setting of silverware inside the stockings and set them next to each person's dinner plate.

*Bargello Christmas Mini Stocking Chart*

# *Bargello Christmas Mini Stocking*

Designed and stitched by Sally London

The finished stocking is 6" long by 4" wide at the toe. Cut 18 count canvas 8"x 10". You will use size 22 tapestry needles and stretcher bars or a small scroll frame.

Fibers used are from Rainbow Gallery. You will need one card each of:
Neon Rays N02-White
Treasure Ribbon Petite PR02-Arctic Gold
Petite Frosty Rays PY026-Christmas Green Gloss
Artic Rays AR12-Red

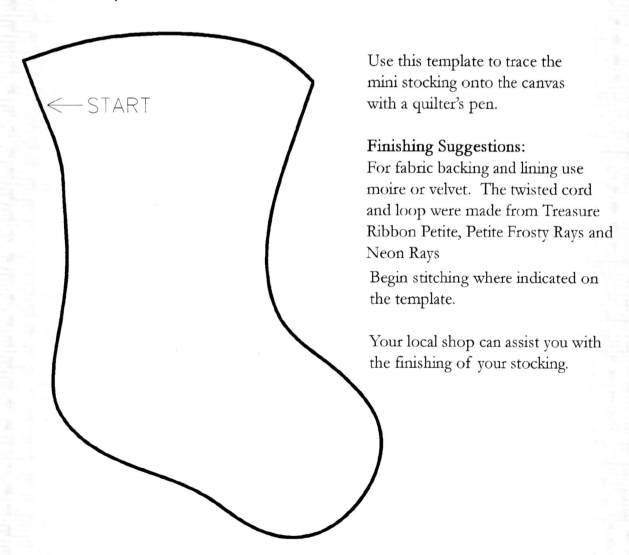

Use this template to trace the mini stocking onto the canvas with a quilter's pen.

**Finishing Suggestions:**
For fabric backing and lining use moire or velvet. The twisted cord and loop were made from Treasure Ribbon Petite, Petite Frosty Rays and Neon Rays

Begin stitching where indicated on the template.

Your local shop can assist you with the finishing of your stocking.

# PROJECT THIRTEEN
## *Childs's Chair One*
### *COLOR FIGURE 32 (BACK COVER)*

Stitched by Susan Seabright

Chair One is a diagonal Chevron design. The Mini Christmas stocking and the border of the Dragon picture also employ variations of this type of design. You can start the design line either in the upper left hand corner of your canvas or, you can center the sixth stitch of the first line of eleven over the center holes of the canvas. The diagonal Chevron can easily be altered by changing the length of the long row or by adding more or less of the small peaks and by making those peaks larger or smaller.

This chair is stitched entirely in Silk & Cream on 14 count brown Mono canvas. Cut your canvas 17"x 19" This is the perfect fiber for a chair seat as it wears well.

<u>Colors of Silk and Cream from Rainbow Gallery.</u>
   Design Line, One skein, shown in **black**, BG33-Burgundy
   One Skein, shown in **dark gray**, BG47-Dark Red
   One Skein, shown in **gray**, BG30-Christmas Red
   One skein, shown in **thin dark gray**, BG32-Pale Peach
   One skein, shown in **white**, BG39-Pale Yellow
   One skein, shown in **gray** ellipse, BG25-Maize
   One skein, shown in **white** ellipse, BG34-White

See Childs Chair One chart on the following page.

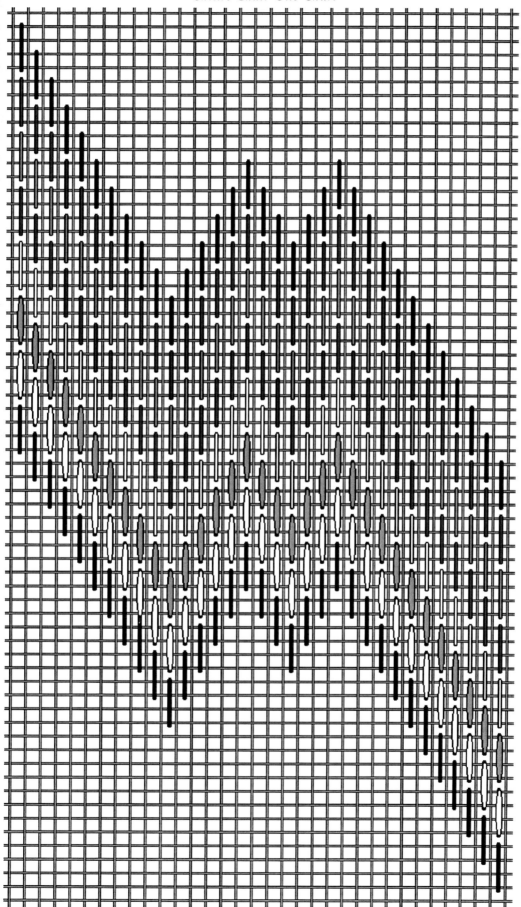

# PROJECT FOURTEEN
## *Childs Chair Two*
### *COLOR FIGURE 32 (BACK COVER)*

Stitched by Susan Seabright

ChairTwo is stitched in the basic Chevron pattern in shades of Taupe on 14 count brown Mono Canvas. Cut your canvas 17"x 19". You will begin with the design line in your darkest shade.

The fibers in this project are distributed by Brown Paper Packages.

<u>Silk & Ivory</u>:
> One Skein, Color 85-Mocha, Shown in **black**
> Two Skeins, Color 26-Mudstone, Shown in **dark gray**
> Two Skeins, Color 08-Taupe, Shown in **gray**
> One Skein, Color 07-Sand, Shown in white **stripe**

See Child's Chair Two chart on following page.

If you are interested in covering a chair that you have at home, you need to make a template of the seat to be covered. This means removing the chair seat and tracing all around the edges. Then add at least three inches all around for the upholstering. If your seat is 8"x 8" you will stitch a piece that is 14" x 14" and you will cut your canvas 18" x 18". Since you are working on a frame, your Bargello seat cover will rarely need to be blocked. Unless you are skilled at recovering furniture, take the seat cover to an upholsterer. You will want to have fresh padding underneath the Bargello as well as fresh muslin. If you order one of these chairs from your needlepoint shop, the shop might make your template.

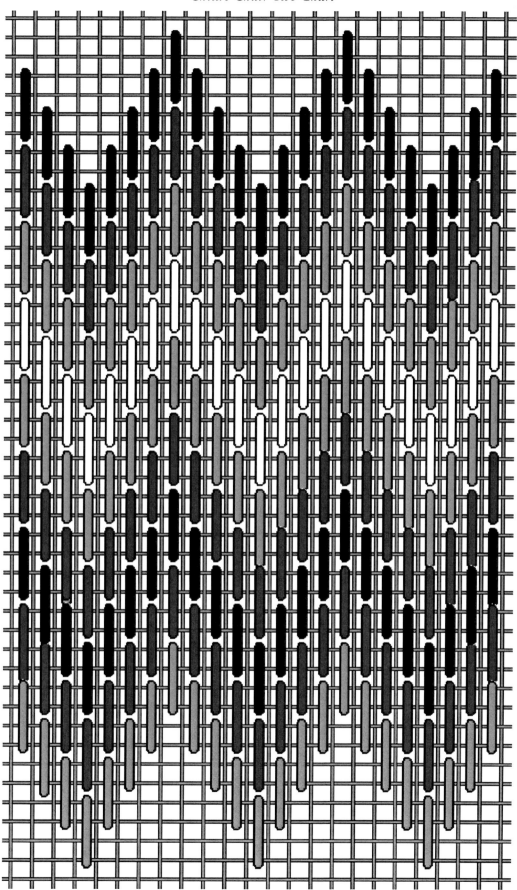

## PROJECT FIFTEEN
# *Childs's Chair Three*
### *COLOR FIGURE 32 (BACK COVER)*

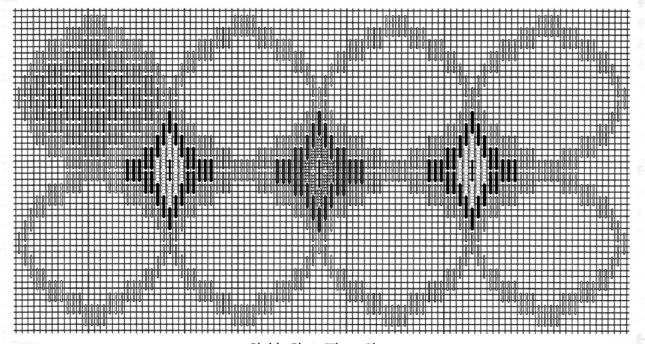

Stitched by Susan Seabright

Chair Three is also stitched in Silk & Ivory from Brown Paper Packages on 14 count brown Mono canvas. Cut your canvas 17"x 19" It is a classic medallion and diamond design. We have previously discussed making the ovals larger or smaller. When you do, the diamonds will automatically be altered

The Design line: one skein, shown in **white**-color 135-Boxwood

Shading Medallions:
> One skein, shown in **gray**-color 38-Eucalyptus
> One skein, shown in **dark gray**-color 45-Willow
> One skein, shown in **black**-color 05-Blue Moon

Shading Diamond One:
> One skein, shown in **thick black**-color 123-Crab
> One skein, shown in **circles**-color 125-Salmon
> One skein, shown in **thin black**-color 11-Really Red

Shading Diamond Two
> One skein, shown in **thick dark gray**-color 04-Peach
> One skein, shown in **triangles**-color 123-Crab
> One skein, shown in **thin dark gray**-color 27-Adobe

*Childs Chair Three Chart*

# PROJECT SIXTEEN
## The Sudberry Long Black Box
### COLOR FIGURE 22

Box Size: 4" x 11"

The design on this box is stitched with Impressions® by Caron. This is a silk/wool blend that fits an 18 count Brown Mono canvas. Cut your canvas to 8" x 15". Below is the list of colors used-from dark to light. I have graphed the design line on the chart below. By now you know how to shade a moiré pattern. This design line, stitched in the lightest purple color, is one of the Hungarian Point patterns. All stitches go over six threads with a step up or down of one thread.

**Use two strands in your needle.**
Colors of Impressions® are:
>    One skein dark purple-color 6040
>    One skein purple-color 6042
>    One skein light purple-color 6043
>    One skein lightest purple-color 6044

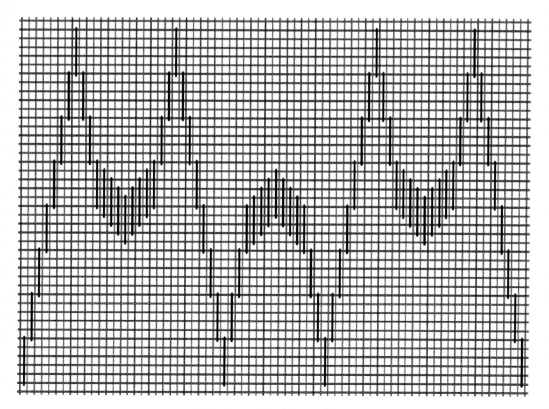

*The Long Black Box Chart*

## ACCESSORIES

Lee's Needle Art, Inc. makes lovely leather purses and accessories. Susan Seabright has stitched all of the following items. She wanted to try Bargello on even-weave fabrics from Zweigart®. I told her to be my guest since I no longer have the eyes for small count fabrics. It was a challenge and she was up for it. The red zip top clutch is stitched on eighteen count Cork Linen. If you do not wish to use the linen, use 18 count white Mono canvas. If you do not want to use an a 18 count material, you can use a larger size. You will have to adjust the pattern accordingly. Use your graph paper before stitching.

## PROJECT SEVENTEEN
# *Red Zip Top Clutch*
### Lee's Needle Art, Inc.  BAG27AR  8" x 4.5"
### *COLOR FIGURE 8*

Stitched by Susan Seabright on Cork Linen, 18 count even-weave fabric. Even if you do not want a purse or cosmetic bag, try these two patterns. They are interesting uses of different length stitches within the Bargello framework.

Weeks Dye Works Over-Dyed Perle Cotton, shown in **gray**, color 4119-Independence
DMC Pearl Cotton #5, shown in **black**, color 336-Navy
DMC Pearl Cotton #5, shown in **white**, color 817- Red

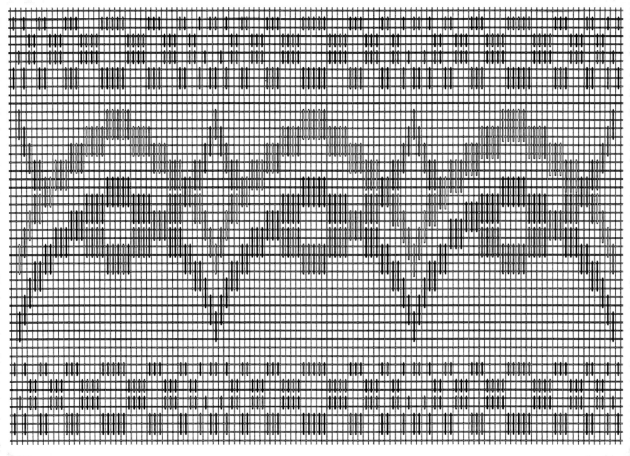

*Red Zip Top Clutch*

# PROJECT EIGHTEEN
## *Brown Alligator City Bag*
### *COLOR FIGURE 16*

Lee's Needle Art, Inc.  #BAG25AB 13"x 7"x 4"
Stitched by Susan Seabright on 18 count Brown Mono Canvas.

The bag is a chevron design with a twist.  The chevrons diminish in size as they move across the design line.  In order to accomplish this, Susan had to change the length of the stitches.  This approach is unusual in Bargello design, so pay strict attention to the chart below.  Do all the design lines first and the rest will follow along in order.  The first chart is the design line only with the color sequence along the border from top to bottom.  Since we want you to start in the middle, you need the count down to set the first line of chevron diamonds, so follow the border guide.  The second chart is the upper quarter of the design.  The rest of the design is the repeat of this quarter.

The brown floss used in this purse is a lovely Egyptian Cotton from Spain called Presencia.  If you are unable to find a shop that carries this stock, I have included alternative DMC colors.

The Materials used:
   Design Line shown in **Black**-Kreinik Tapestry Braid.  One spool of #12-C02.
   Use 8 threads of the Embroidery Floss in your needle of the colors shown on the color chart:

The color chart is on the following page.

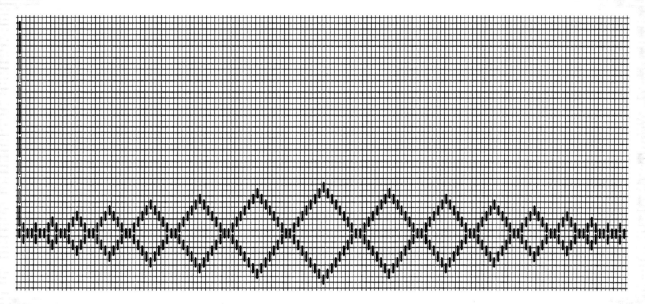

*Brown Alligator City Bag Design Line*

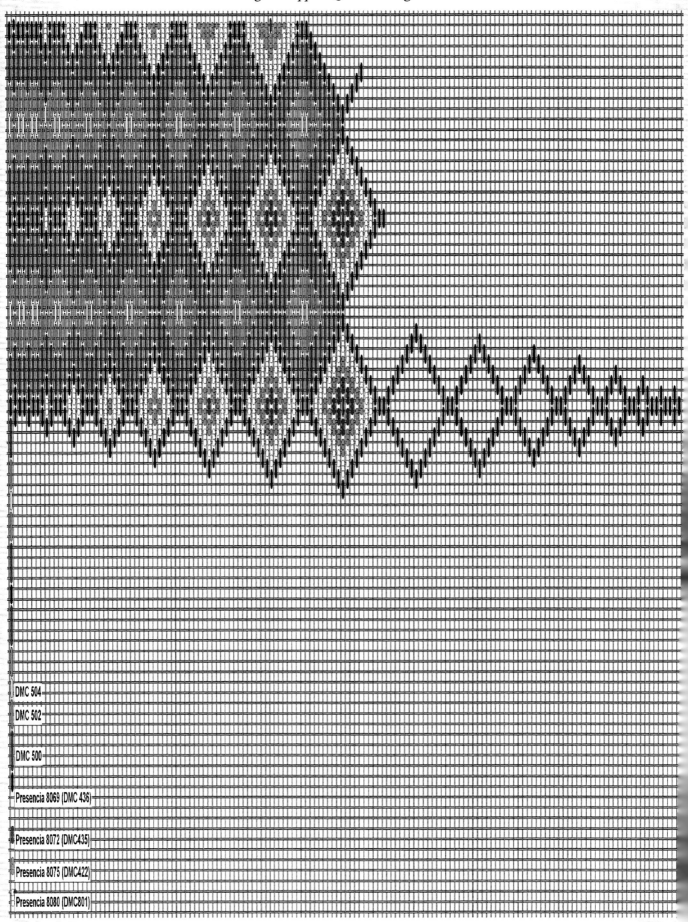

DMC 504

DMC 502

DMC 500

Presencia 8069 (DMC 436)

Presencia 8072 (DMC435)

Presencia 8075 (DMC422)

Presencia 8080 (DMC801)

# PROJECT NINETEEN
## *Green Cosmetic Bag*
### *COLOR FIGURE 7*

Lee's Needle Art, Inc.  #BAG22AG  8"x 5" x 2"
Stitched by Susan Seabright
Stitched on 18 Brown Mono Canvas

Design Line shown in **black**, J.L .Walsh 50/50 silk & wool, color 3368
Shown in dark **gray**, J.L .Walsh 50/50 silk & wool, color 3366
Shown in **gray**, J.L.  Walsh 50/50 silk & wool, color 3325
Shown in **white**, Rainbow Gallery Very Velvet™ V220-Yellow

*Green Cosmetic Bag Chart*

# PROJECT TWENTY
## *Watch Band*
### *COLOR FIGURE 17*

The watch band is done in a simple Double Brick Stitch. If you purchase the watch, you will receive the canvas, findings, all finishing materials and instructions. You may choose to use any fibers that fit number 18 white Mono canvas.

The thread I used is Snipits by Stitch Elegance; a variegated hand dyed mercerized cotton.
Lightest color, Lavender Blue
Middle color, Grape
Darkest color, Deep Water

I started with the lightest color and used one strand of the fiber. I then used the middle color and followed with the darkest. You may find that you would prefer two strands of the fiber for more coverage.

*Watch Band Chart*

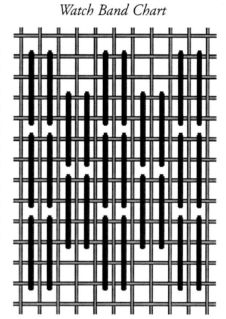

Watch bands, camera straps, belts, purse straps, luggage straps, napkin rings, curtain tie backs, or any other straps are quick and easy Bargello projects. Ovals in a row, chevrons and diamonds, make beautiful linear designs. Your needlepoint shop can finish any of these items. Some shops carry luggage racks and belt buckles. If your shop does not, it is not hard to find any of these items elsewhere. If you have a sport watch that could use some perking up, carefully remove the old band and use it to measure your new one. Your shop should have a finisher who can complete your watch band.

# PROJECTS TWENTY-ONE AND TWENTY-TWO
## *The Sudberry Music Box*
### 2 3/4" X 1 3/4"   *COLOR FIGURE 2*
## *The Sudberry Oak Ring Box #99308*
### 3"X 3"   *COLOR FIGURE 3*

Both projects are stitched on 18 count Brown Mono canvas.

   The material is over-dyed Perle Cotton from Crescent colors.
   The design line is shown in **white**, one skein of color- La Tierra
   One skein, shown in **dark gray,** color-Country Lane
   One skein, shown in **light gray,** color-Toasted Marshmallow
   One skein, shown in **black,** color-Eves' Leaves.  This is a very subtle variegated green.

The Ring Box uses the same colors and symbols as the Music Box.  This is a small Four-Way Bargello design.  Both designs leave the backgrounds open.  Bargello designs lend themselves to this option.  The open canvas tends to compliment the long, raised Bargello stitches.  If you do not agree, just fill in the background with basket weave.  You will get the same raised effect.

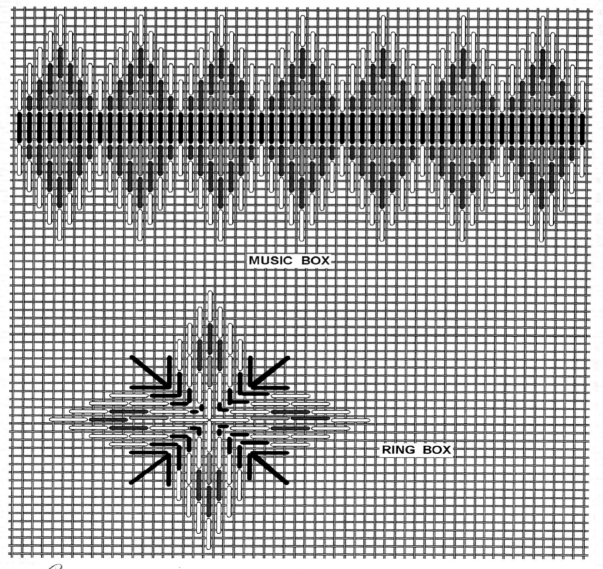

MUSIC BOX

RING BOX

# PROJECT TWENTY THREE
## *Susan's Sudberry House Tray*
### 11"x 11"   *COLOR FIGURE 15*

Design Size 9 1/2"x 9 1/2" Cut 14 count brown Mono canvas 14"x 14"

This design is a mirror image two-way Bargello. This is Susan's design and her description. The design reverses at the middle to form the small center motif. The design then repeats below the center in mirror image style. Your chart is one quarter of the design. I have included the top and bottom starting point for the repeat and the mirror image. Susan used two strands of Impressions by Caron in the following colors:

Design line shown in Black stripe-Color #8020, Darkest Green
Line shown in Dark Gray stripe-Color #8022, Dark Green
Line shown in Gray stripe-Color #8024,Middle Green
Line shown in White triangles-Color #8026, Light Green
Line shown in White stripe-Color#8027, Lightest Green
Line shown in Black triangles-Color #1122, Darkest Brown
Line shown in Dark Gray triangles-Color #1130, Dark Brown
Line shown in Gray triangles-Color #1131, Darker Middle Brown
Line shown in Gray circles-Color #1134, Middle Brown
Line shown in White circles-Color #1136, Light Brown
Line shown in White Squares-Color #1139, Lightest Brown

*Small Square Tray*

# PROJECT TWENTY FOUR
## Susan's Sudberry House
## #95311 Walnut Trivet
### DESIGN SIZE 5"X 5"  COLOR FIGURE 19

Cut 18 count brown canvas 9" x 9" as you will need extra canvas to roll around the mounting square that is included. Instructions for finishing are provided.

This is an innovative design. Susan wanted to achieve a pleasing curved and woven design line that fit into the required area. She altered the count and length of the stitches until she had the desired effect. Susan could not decide which of the Gumnut colors she wanted to use so she stitched them all. I have not charted all the colors since I thought this would be confusing. You will find the sequence for the fill on the last row of the chart. If you study the picture, you will see the progression of colors. The fibers used are as follows:

"Jewels" Silk Pearl from Gumnut Yarns
Turquoise-Medium                     Sapphire-Dark
Ruby-Light                           Amethyst-Light
Sapphire-Light                       Amethyst-Medium
Sapphire-Medium                      Amethyst-Dark

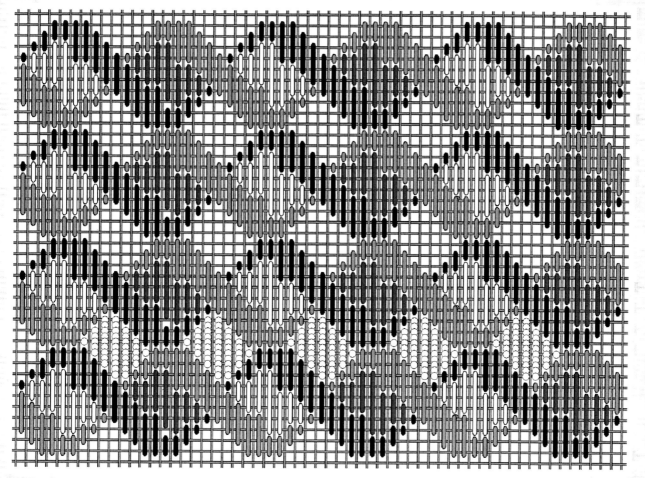

This is the end of the section featuring projects. Among these projects are many design lines that you can use in untold number of ways. Take the charts apart, resize them, expand them and change the colors. I wish you many hours of happy stitching. If you would like to share your designs with me, I would be delighted to see them. Who knows, you could be a part of the next book or, even better, in a book of your own. A good teacher, like a good gardener, wants to see her students grow and blossom. You will find my E-mail address on the last page of this book, titled *In Conclusion*.

## *Possibilities*

The following pieces are pictures in the color section, and are examples of what happens when you begin to experiment with Bargello designs. If all goes well, Susan and I will be collaborating on a second book. She has already stitched these pieces of advanced Bargello design. Use the colored pictures as guides to your own explorations into stitching and designing Bargello.

## *Beyond Bargello*
### THE DESIGNS OF SUSAN SEABRIGHT

**Susan's Sudberry House Small Square Box** is stitched on cork linen using DMC floss and variegated floss. This is an asymmetrical Bargello design which you may view in the color section, *color figure 18*. It is a truly original design. We want to give you a preview of what is to come. but as this is a complicated design, we will explore the technique used in the next book.

**Susan's Childs Corner Chair** is pictured in the color section, *color figure 28.* This wonderful chair is distributed by Needle Art Furniture. The cushion is stitched in a Four-Way Bargello pattern. There are two Four-Way patterns in this book. There is a book on Four-Way designs that you will find on the book list. The thread used is J.L Walsh 50/50 silk & wool.

**Susan's Little Jewel Box** appears in the color section, *color figure 9.* This project is done on tiny 30 count even-weave fabric. It is a Four-Way pattern split in two. We will discuss this unique pattern in the next book.

**Iona's Pictorial Triptych** appears in the color section, *color figures 23, 24 & 25*. They are exercises in invoking a mood. The pictures are called "Mountain Sunrise", "Seaside Sunset" and "High Desert Stars". They were originally published by Rainbow Gallery, and we thank them for permission to use them.

**Iona's Little Dragon,** _color figure 11_, illustrates the use of Bargello (diagonal Chevrons) as a border around a Needlepoint canvas. I often use a mitered Bargello pattern instead of mat board when framing my pictures.

**Iona's Free Form Bargello Footstool** appears in the color section in _color figure 32_. I have been told that this is an original method of coloring a Bargello pattern. I won't claim that distinction since very few methods are original after all the centuries of needle work. The thread used is Paternayan Persian Wool. This is still the yarn of choice for those items that will be stepped on or sat upon. This stool has been used in our house for many years, and it still looks fresh and vibrant.

## *The Needle Artistry of Ruth Dilts*
### COLOR FIGURE 29

Ruth is a wonderful friend of mine. She has taught me many things over the years and on the way we manage to have a lot of fun. Ruth is a very talented designer and accomplished teacher. She has been kind enough to lend me some of her designs to feature in this book. She used many threads from many sources. If I have not indicated the source of the thread than you can assume that it is a Rainbow Gallery product. Some of these designs are totally Bargello pieces and some combine Bargello with other techniques. All of them are lovely. If you would like to try stitching any of these designs you can reach Ruth at:

Ruth Dilts
9400 William Kirk Lane
Burke, VA. 22015
Phone: 703-455-7047
E-Mail- ruthdiltsdesign@cox.net.

## THE CHRISTMAS BALLS

The Florence© Christmas Ball is an intriguing four-way Bargello design which looks great in the round. The threads used here are Flair, Petite Very Velvet, Rainbow Cashmere, Patina and Treasure Braid from Rainbow Gallery, and Watercolours from Caron. Ruth gives you detailed instructions on finishing the ball, although, most needle work shops will be able to finish it for you.

The Hagerstown© Christmas Ball combines Florentine Point Bargello with a quick and easy darning stitch background. The threads used are Kreinik Braid and blending filament combined with Anchor, or DMC six strand embroidery floss. Ruth signs off her charts with the phrase "Have Fun". I think these balls are fun and there are eight of them. Imagine what a Christmas tree decorated with needlepoint Christmas balls would look like! Gorgeous I am sure.

## THE PILLOWS

The "Diamonds are a Girl's Best Friend©" pillow is a design featuring Four-Way Bargello medallions paired with Florentine Point medallions floating on a field of darning stitches on 18 count canvas. The threads used in the pillow include Bravo, Flair, Patina, Pebbly Perle, Rainbow Linen, and Splendor Silk. This is quite a line-up of diverse threads. Ruth, like the great teacher that she is, includes instructions on using the fibers as well as finishing the pillow yourself.

The Victorian Ribbons© pillow is a visually stunning piece. I wanted you to see this since the pillow is a perfect example of Bargello combined with other needlepoint techniques. Ruth has taught this design many times and it is a mini-course in elegant stitchery. The threads used in this pillow include Splendor Silk, Elegance Silk Pearl, Kreinik #4 Braid, Wildflowers and Impressions by Caron as well as Mill Hill Beads.

The Lily Langtree© roll pillow is, like the pillow above, a project that combines Hungarian Point Bargello with many other lovely needlepoint techniques. The threads used in this design are Splendor Silk, Elegance Silk Pearl, Kreinik #4 Braid, Wildflowers and Impressions by Caron as well as DMC #8 Pearl Cotton and Mill Hill Beads.

## *Paul Krynicki of River Silks Ltd.*
### COLOR FIGURES 27, 30 & 31

Samples stitched by Lynn Krynick Bayer.

Paul's wild and wonderful fibers can be seen in the color section. You will find information on his products in the chapter on fibers. River Silk is a ribbon that comes in three sizes and over 290 colors. The ribbons are all hand dyed and I think that you can see by the color photos that they are very unusual. You can get kits for many of River Silks projects from your local needlework shop. Susan and I are looking forward to using these silk ribbons in the next book.

# CHAPTER SEVEN
## *Fibers Available to Today's Needlework Artist*

Most fibers come with a tag, card or an identifying band. You should read these as they contain a wealth of information on the fibers themselves. Some cards or tags will tell you whether the fiber is colorfast, what blend of materials are in the fiber, or how many threads make up a strand. It may state country of origin and what canvas mesh will work the best with each fiber. All fibers come with an identifying name or number. Often the dye lot number is included. Always save this tag or card along with a small sample of the fiber. This way you always know what color and dye lot you are using.

Below you will find a listing of the fibers and materials that were used in this book. You will also find information that I know about the fiber, and comments on its use. Many of these hints were taught to me by Jay Patterson. Jay has retired from the industry, but his ability and wisdom live on.

I have included the address, phone and fax number as well as the web site and E-mail if available, of the manufacturers and distributors of the materials used in the book. If you would like to use any of these materials, contact your local shop or check with the supplier for a shop close to you.

## *BEAU GESTE, INC.*
4407 N. Racine Avenue #1
Chicago, IL 60640
Phone: 800-344-5542
Web: www.beaugestedesigns.com          E-Mail: info@beaugestedesigns.com

### *Wonder Twist*
100% Nylon Colorfast but test first.
Use 1 or 2 ply on 24 count needlepoint canvas and 1 or 2 ply on 13 to 18 count canvas. Use a #22 or #20 tapestry needle for best results. Wonder Twist is a lively, shiny nylon twist that comes in 75 bright and crisp colors, including 14 colors with a metallic twist added and 11 variegated colors.

---

## *BROWN PAPER PACKAGES*
3730 Alexandria Pike
Cold Spring, KY 41076
Phone: 859-441-4421  Fax 859-441-4103
Web: www.brownpaperpackages.com          E-Mail: bpp@one.net

### *Silk & Ivory*
50% Silk and 50% Merino Wool. Hand Washable; test first.
Fits 12 to 14 count needlepoint canvas.
This lovely material comes from Switzerland. Merino wool is one of the world's finest wools, and it is reflected in the soft feel of this thread. The silk lends a soft glow and strength to the fiber. I love Silk & Ivory and I am sure that you will too. This is a sturdy fiber and you may use a slightly longer length.

### THE CARON COLLECTION
55 Old South Avenue
Stratford, CT 06615
Phone: 203-381-9999  Fax: 203-381-9003
Web: www.caron-net.com                    E-Mail: mail@caron-net.com

#### Impressions by Caron
50% Silk, 50% Wool-Colorfast but test first..
Fits 13 count to 18 count needlepoint canvas, and 18 count brown Mono canvas. When you purchase this product be sure to read the tag. There is a wealth of information on the inside. This silk/wool blend is imported from Italy. It is the thinnest of the silk/wool blends used in this book. Like the other blends, it is strong, yet soft and easy to work with. Be sure that the two strands lie flat on the canvas. The Caron collection also offers Watercolours®, Wildflowers® and Waterlilies®. You would enjoy using these fine threads in your projects.

---

### CRESCENT COLOURS
4100 S. Fremont Ave. Ste.100
Tucson, AZ 85714
Phone: 520-741-1950  Fax: 520-744-0195
Web: www.crescentcolours.com                    E-Mail: sales@crescentcolours.com

#### Over-dyed Perle Cotton
100% Cotton; Hand dyed. Test first. Use on 14 to 18 count canvas.
The examples in this book are stitched in over-dyed Perle Cotton. Crescent also dyes six-strand embroidery floss. I like the crisp look of this product as well as the very-very subtle color changes. This is a great fiber to use in a Bargello project. Don't cut too long a strand because polished cotton will loose its luster.

---

### CUSTOM HOUSE OF NEEDLE ARTS
Distributor of Gumnut Yarns
154 Weir St.
Glastonbury, CT 06033-2950
Phone: 860-633-2950                    Fax: 860-633-2950
Web: www.customhouseofneedlearts.com        E-Mail: customhouse@aol.com

#### Jewels
100% Australian Over-Dyed Silk Pearl
Use a double strand on 14 count brown Mono canvas.
The threads used in the trivet are six different shades of Jewels. The colors are very muted and subtle. The thread is about the size of #8 Pearl Cotton and is very versatile. Since it is a crewel weight material, you may use as many plies as needed to cover a variety of canvas sizes. There are a wide variety of colors and styles in this line as well as several lines of wool threads. The fibers are made in Australia.

## THE DMC CORPORATION
77 South Hackensack Avenue
Port Kearny Bldg. 10F
South Kearny, NJ 07032-4688                    Web: www.DMC.com

*Six Strand Embroidery Floss* (Art. 117) Strandable-fits any size material or evenweave canvas. 100% double mercerized long staple cotton. DMC threads are colorfast. DMC is the oldest corporation in the world. You can find their products anywhere and most certainly at your local shop. The alligator purse is stitched with 8 strands of floss. Susan's Sudberry box is stitched with new DMC **Color** *Variations Embroidery Floss* (Art. 417). The multi-colors are dyed with combinations of DMC Colors allowing them to coordinate with one another as they do on this box design.

---

## KREINIK MANUFACTURING CO. INC.
P.O. Box 1966
Parkersburg, WV 26102-1966
Phone: 800-537-2166 Fax: 304-428-4326
Web: www.Kreinik.com                    E-Mail: info@kreinik.com

### Kreinik Metallic
#12 Tapestry™ Braid stitches nicely into 18 count Brown Mono Canvas. Kreinik metallic braids are made of imported polyester/viscose filaments. Kreinik manufactures a wide variety of metallic threads, round and flat braids, as well as, several lines of silk threads.

---

## PRESENCIA USA, INC.
P.O. Box 2409
Evergreen, CO 80437-2409
Phone: 866-277-6364 Fax: 303-670-2179
Web: www.presenciausa.com                    E-Mail: info@presenciausa.com

### Presencia/Finca
A fine Egyptian Cotton 6-strand floss manufactured in Spain. It is a soft lustrous Mouline dyed in colors that blend well with other Embroidery Floss.

---

## RAINBOW GALLERY
7412 Fulton Ave. #5
North Hollywood, CA 91605
Phone: 818-982-6406 Fax: 818-982-1476
Web: www.rainbowgallery.com                    E-Mail: info@rainbowgallery.com

### Arctic Rays
Fits a 14 to 18 count canvas. Use a full strand on 18 count canvas.
There are pieces of transparent fiber woven into the thread that give Arctic Rays a glistening effect. It is suggested that you use a larger than usual needle to enlarge the canvas holes so that the fiber will stitch without shredding. The longer stitches of Bargello will allow for maximum effect as the fringes will not be hidden.

### Backgrounds
Helene is a 100% natural silk thread. The Background line of fibers includes six natural silk and linen threads.

### Flair®

100% Nylon.

Fits a 14 to 18 count canvas.

Flair is one of the most versatile needlepoint materials I have ever come across. It has a soft glisten when added to a canvas. It enhances, but does not overpower, other fibers. The only problem with Flair is that it will unravel while you are working. You must pay attention to the end of the thread in the eye of your needle. If it starts to unravel, you will see a tiny thread. Just trim the tail and keep stitching. Another "rule of thumb" is to always cut this fiber at a severe angle. Bargello stitches are easier on Flair than Basketweave since you are stitching straight up and down on a frame. Use a laying tool to keep the ribbon flat.

### Frosty Rays® and Petite Frosty Rays®

78% Nylon, 14% Rayon, 8% Polyester

Fits a 12 to 18 count canvas. Use a full strand of Frosty Rays on 14 count canvas, and Petite Frosty Rays on 18 count canvas. This fiber is a Nylon tube with a Metalized Polyester thread inside. This is one of my all time Bargello favorites. Be very sure to cut this fiber on an angle. When you take Frosty Rays off the card and cut it, the fill metallic will be loosely coiled within the tube. Hold one end and pull it taut. Make sure you are holding both fibers. Cut this and all ribbons at an angle. The fill fiber will slip as you stitch, and you will have to trim the end now and then to prevent it from catching. You will like the look of Frosty Rays much better if you use a laying tool while stitching.

### Fyre Werks®

Fits a 12 to 18 count canvas.

This lovely metallic ribbon is another one of my favorites. It is highly reflective and will add "pizzazz" to any project. The ends of the ribbon tend to fray and you will not be able to stitch with most of the tail in the eye of the needle. Aside from that, Fyre Werks is a very sturdy ribbon that, like all ribbons, looks best when laying flat on the canvas. So use your laying tool or your finger to keep it straight. Yes, I did say finger. Stiffer ribbons like Fyre Werks are easy to control with your fingers while working. Do not cut overly long lengths and **do** cut on an angle.

### Neon Rays®

100% Hand Washable Rayon Ribbon; test first before wetting.

Fits a 12 to 18 count canvas. Use a full strand on 14 count canvas.

Neon Rays comes off the card with pronounced kinks. Do not try to stitch with these kinks. Run the working thread over a damp sponge. The thread dries almost instantly. You could iron the thread, but who would want to? If you do, be careful not to stretch the thread thin. You could also use a clean hot light bulb, but again, the damp sponge is so easy. You must use a laying tool with this fiber to keep it from twisting. Use a loose rather than tight tension while stitching. Use a longer tail and the Bargello tuck or "J" ending at all times. Rayon is very slippery. Cut Neon Rays at an angle. I know that Rayon has a bad reputation among some needle workers, but don't be hesitant. If you follow the procedures mentioned above, you will add a lovely accent to all your future projects.

### Overture®

100% Hand Washable Over Dyed Cotton; test first before wetting.

Fits a 12 to 18 count canvas. Use a full strand on 14 count canvas. If you find this too thick, just remove one strand. Overture is a 4 stranded fiber. Each strand is about the size of Pearl Cotton #5. When you are stitching a line of Bargello with an over Dyed fiber, you need to pay attention to the order of your colors in order to ensure a smooth transition from shade to shade. I always cut in the center of a color passage. Then, when I cut the next length, the working end or tail of the thread is next off the card or skein. The end threaded in the eye of the needle is the end that contains a new color. Cut a normal length of thread to preserve the finish of this fiber.

### Rainbow Tweed

44% Cotton, 39% Wool, 17% Acrylic, Hand Washable; test first before wetting. Four-ply fits 13 to 16 count canvas. 2 ply fits eighteen count canvas. Rainbow Tweed comes in both solid and variegated colors. It is a four ply fiber that is a pleasure to use. It fits 14 count canvas perfectly. It is strong and resists fraying. Therefore, you can cut a slightly longer strand. This tweed is the perfect fiber for coats, tree trunks, earth and any other natural objects.

### Razzle-Dazzle 6®

70% Nylon; 30% Metalized Polyester, Hand Washable. Test first before wetting. Fits a 12 to 14 count canvas. This fiber is a gem for Bargello. Its rough texture is caused by the thin strand of Metalized Polyester that is wound around the Nylon thread. It makes the fiber sparkle and gives it the well deserved name-Razzle-Dazzle. This is one thread that you will want to poke stitch with even if you are not using a frame (which you should be doing).

### Silk & Cream

50% Wool and 50% Silk
Fits a 14 to 18 count canvas. Use a full strand on 18 count canvas. This is a wonderful fiber for needlepoint. Stitching with Silk & Cream is effortless. The fiber has a quiet glow that compliments other materials. I use Silk & Cream for needlepoint backgrounds and for Bargello projects, not only because it looks beautiful, but also because the stitches work up quickly and the fiber maintains its integrity even when using slightly longer lengths.

### Sparkle Rays

97% Polyester, 3% Nylon; hand Washable. Test first before wetting.
Fits a 12 to 14 count canvas. Sparkle Rays is a woven ribbon with metallic filaments woven into it. This makes it a very easy thread to stitch with. As always, a laying tool is strongly suggested, especially, if you want to emphasize the lovely, quiet sparkle of this lovely ribbon. This is another of my Bargello favorites.

### Very Velvet™ and Petite Very Velvet™

100% Nylon, Hand Washable; test first before wetting.
Fits a 12 to 18 count canvas. Very Velvet has a nylon cord at its center. If you are not careful while threading Very Velvet, you could damage the fiber. Here is what I do. I always use a needle threader. I leave a small tail. After a few stitches you will see a notch form in the thread. The needle stays in the notch and you do not have to worry about losing your needle or damaging your thread. I love the texture of this fiber. It adds a soft matte look to your project and is very easy to use. If you are planning on using an eighteen count canvas, you will want to use Petite Very Velvet.

### Water N' Ice

100% Nylon, Hand Washable; test first before wetting.

Fits a 12 to 18 count canvas. This is a very clever fiber. Water N' Ice is semi transparent except for the dark colors which have a wonderful wet look. You can use it to stitch a mirror, window, water or, of course, ice. You can also use it as I did in Winter Wonder. It serves to create a feeling of winter. This material also comes in the colors of sunshine and fire as well as Halloween pumpkins. It is easy to use and a great problem solver for difficult effects. I have seen the white version of Water N' Ice stitched over an entire painted canvas. The painting shows through and the canvas has a stained glass window effect.

---

## RIVER SILKS LTD.

11215 NE 58th Place
Kirkland, WA. 98033
Phone: 425-827-3972  Fax: 425-739-6003
Web: www.riversilks.com                E-Mail: ribbons@riversilks.com

This beautiful silk ribbon was developed in Suzhou, China, the silk capitol of the world. The ribbon is finely woven with an almost imperceptible selvage edge. This product is very strong and resists running and tearing. There are a over 290 hand dyed colors which are available in 4mm and 7mm widths, and 70 colors in 13mm widths. Each spool contains 5.5 yards of ribbon.

---

## STITCH ELEGANCE

5617 Crowndale Dr.
Plano, TX. 75093-6746
Phone: 972-403-0431   Fax: 972-473-6746
Web: www.stitchelegance.com                E-Mail: lisa.willis@stitchelegance.com

### Snipits

100% Mercerized Cotton. Hand-dyed, but it is colorfast because of multiple rinsing. Fits 18 count canvas for Needlepoint and Bargello. I enjoy stitching with this cotton. It is a little less lustrous than Perle cotton and just perfect for the watch that is illustrated in the color section.

---

## J.L. WALSH SILK

4338 Edgewood Avenue
Oakland, CA  94602
Phone: 510-530-7343                E-Mail: barrere@ix.netcom.com

### Silk/Wool

59% Silk, 50% Wool; hand washable. Test first.

Fits a 14 count brown Mono canvas. This Silk-Wool was used on the seat of the corner chair that is illustrated in the color section. This is a Four-Way Bargello. Walsh's Silk/Wool blend is a big fluffy braided fiber and is wonderful to work with. All of JL Walsh silks are hand dyed in exquisite and unusually vivid, vibrant colors.

## WEEKS DYE WORKS
1510-103 Mechanical Blvd.
Garner, NC. 27529
Phone: 919-772-9166 Fax: 919-772-8757
Web: www.weeksdyeworks.com          E-Mail: Miranda@weeksdyeworks.com

Hand over-dyed Cotton Embroidery Floss and Pearl Cotton in sizes #3, 5, 8. This company offers a unusual selection of beautiful colors. The color families are long and well suited for stitching Bargello projects.

---

## WILTEX THREADS, INC.
433 Beacon Street
Suite 2F
Boston, MA 02115
Phone: 917-822-9359 Fax: 617-262-1236
Web: www.vineyardsilk.com          E-Mail: Karen@vineyardsilk.com

### Vineyard Silk Classic
100% non-strandable silk in sizes that fit 13 and 18 count canvas. The silk comes in solid and over-dyed colors. This is a soft silk with a matte finish similar to Perle Cotton. Use short lengths to preserve its glowing finish. There is also a silk thread spun with metallic accents.

---

## ZWEIGART/JOAN TOGGITT LTD.
James Kornecki
262 Old New Brunswick Road Suite E
Piscataway, NJ 08854-3756
Phone: 732-562-8888 Toll Free: 866-993-4427
Web: www.zweigart.com          E-Mail: info@zweigart.com

### NEEDLEPOINT CANVAS & EVENWEAVE MATERIALS
The materials and needlepoint canvas offered by this German Company sets the standard for quality and durability. You will find Zweigart products in most needlework shops. All of the samples in this book were stitched on either Zweigart brown Mono canvas or Zweigart Evenweave materials.

## WHERE TO FIND THE ITEMS SHOWN ON THE COLOR PAGES:

If your local shop does not carry the item that interests you, ask them to order it; or you may contact the supplier listed below for a shop near you who carries the item.

## FURNITURE AND ACCESSORY ITEMS

The Four Chairs:

### *Needle Art Furniture*

219 N. Palestine
Athens, TX 75751-8044
Phone: 903-675-8034  Fax: 903-675-8044
This company specializes in Chippendale, Queen Anne, Louis XV and Louis XVI reproductions of footstools and children's chairs.  See the four chairs pictured in the color section.

## THE BOXES AND TRIVETS

### *Sudberry House, Inc.*

12 Colton Rd.
East Lyme, CT.  06333
Phone: 860-739-6951  Fax: 860-739-9267
Web: www.sudberryhouse.com                E-mail: sales@sudberry.com
The black long box, has been discontinued although there may be a few left in stock at the factory.  The small ring box, the music box, the trivet and the tray are still current items.  Sudberry House products are available at your local needle work shop.

## WATCH

### *L'Esprit De France*

4331 NE Couch St.
Portland, OR  972123-1671
Phone: 503-235-1326  Fax: 503-235-1326
Web: www.lespritdefrance.com                E-Mail: defrance@teleport.com

## PURSES

### *Lee's Needle Art, Inc.*

Robin L.  Clark, Sales Mgr.
5630 Route 38
Pennsauken, New Jersey  08109
Phone: 800-715-6605          Fax: 856-665-3812
Phone: 856-665-8323                E-Mail: leesneedleart@comcast.net

# CHAPTER EIGHT
## *Final Comments*

I hope you have enjoyed this book, and are now inspired to create your own exciting Bargello designs. As I stated in the beginning, that was my goal. There are so many fibers, ideas, and inspirations and they are all out there waiting for you.

Susan and I are already talking about a second book that, right now, we refer to as "Beyond Bargello". She has thought of several ideas that I would never have imagined in a million years. This will be a book of projects that we hope will push the envelope of Bargello design.

Meanwhile, I hope that all of you new designers will be busy stitching. Perhaps you have a new idea, or one that is an intriguing twist on an old pattern. If you do, I would love to see it. If it is something that you created while stitching along with this book, I would be most delighted if you would share it with me. You may e-mail me at rdetidet@sbcglobal.net. I always answer my mail, and I will be happy to help you out with any problems you might have with any project in the book. I am sorry but I cannot accept collect calls. If you do need to reach me, please use the e-mail address.

Thank you for purchasing this book. I hope it inspires you and leads you to the creation of many unique designs. It has been an adventure to write "Creating Contemporary Bargello" and a pleasure to accomplish something that I have wanted to do for so a long time.

Happy Stitching,

Iona L. Dettelbach

## Books you may be interested in reading:

Many of the books on this list are out of print, but are valuable reference books. If your local shop does not have a copy for sale, they may have it as a reference book. It may be available at your local library or may be found on Amazon.com or E-Bay.

***Florentine Embroidery***
Barbara Snook
Charles Scribner's Sons
New York, NY
ISBN: 0684105608

***The Margaret Boyles Bargello Workbook***
Macmillan Publishing Co. Inc.
866 Third Ave.
New York, NY 10022
ISBN: 0025143301

***Bargello-Florentine Canvas Work***
Elsa S. Williams
Van Nostrand Reinhold Company
450 West 33rd Street
New York, NY 10001
ISBN: 0442112483

***The* Bargello *Book***
Frances Salter
Lacis Publications
3163 Adeline Street
Berkeley, CA 94703
ISBN: 0713679530

***Bargello: An Explosion In Color***
Macmillan Publishing Co., Inc.
866 Third Ave.
New York, NY 10022
ISBN: 0025143204

***Bargello and Related Stitchery***
Charles Barnes and David P. Blake
Hearthside Press
Great Neck, NY 11021
ISBN: 0820803375

***Traditional Bargello***
Dorothy Phelan
St. Martin's Press
175 Fifth Ave.
New York, NY 10010
ISBN: 0312068824

***The Needlepoint Book***
Jo Ippolito Christensen
A Fireside Book
Published by Simon and Schuster
New York, NY 10020
ISBN: 0684832305

***Designs For Bargello***
Nikki Scheuer
Doubleday and Company
New York, NY
ISBN: 0385000669

***Bargello Magic***
Pauline Fischer and Anabel Lasker
Holt Reinhart & Winston, Inc.
383 Madison Ave.
New York, NY 10017
ISBN: 0-03-088259-1

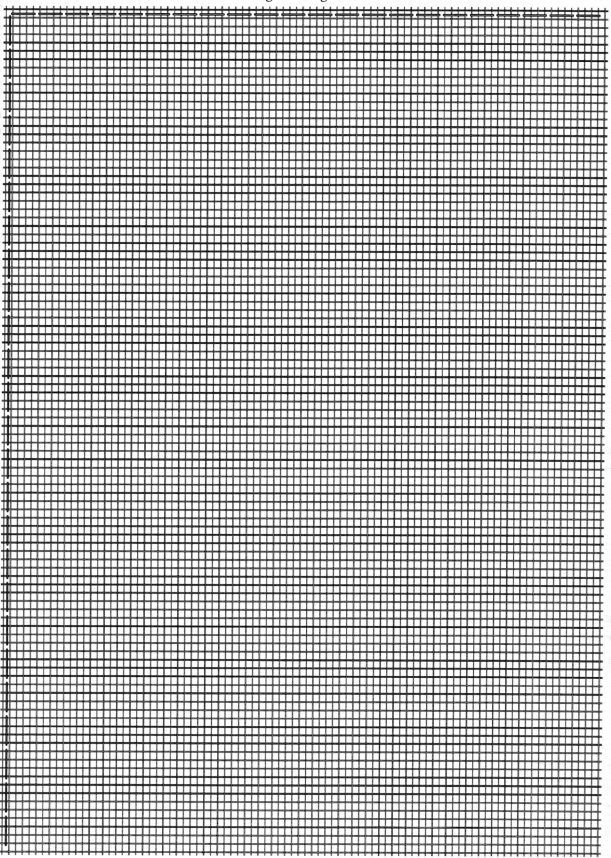

# My Project Notes

Date_____

_____

_____

_____

_____

_____

_____

_____

_____

_____

_____

_____

_____

_____

_____

_____

_____

_____

# My Project Notes

Date_____

_____

_____

_____

_____

_____

_____

_____

_____

_____

_____

_____

_____

_____

_____

_____

_____

_____

_____

_____

# My Project Notes

Date_____

_____

_____

_____

_____

_____

_____

_____

_____

_____

_____

_____

_____

_____

_____

_____

_____

_____

_____

_____